Unreliable Truth:

  On Memoir and Memory

Unreliable Truth:
On Memoir and Memory

Maureen Murdock

SEAL PRESS

Unreliable Truth: *On Memoir and Memory*

HOUSTON PUBLIC LIBRARY

R01238 86991

Copyright © 2003 by Maureen Murdock

Published by
Seal Press
An Imprint of Avalon Publishing Group Incorporated
161 William St., 16th Floor
New York, NY 10038

All permissions notices appear at the end of the book in a separate
Credits section.

All rights reserved. No part of this book may be reproduced or trans-
mitted in any form without written permission from the publisher,
except by reviewers who may quote brief excerpts in connection with a
review.

Library of Congress Cataloging-in-Publication Data is available.

ISBN 1-58005-083-2

9 8 7 6 5 4 3 2 1

Designed by Shona McCarthy
Printed in the United States of America
Distributed by Publishers Group West

To Ella and Gillian,
who carry on our womanline

We wish to assert our existence, like dogs peeing on fire hydrants. We put on display our framed photographs, our parchment diplomas, our silver-plated cups; we monogram our linen, we carve our names on trees, we scrawl them on washroom walls. It's all the same impulse. What do we hope from it? Applause, envy, respect? Or simply attention, of any kind we can get? At the very least we want a witness. We can't stand the idea of our own voices falling silent finally, like a radio running down.

—Margaret Atwood, *The Blind Assassin*

We shall not cease from exploration
And the end of all our exploring
Will be to arrive where we started
And know the place for the first time.

—T. S. Eliot, *Little Gidding*

Contents

PART ONE

To the Best of My Recollection

There Is So Much I Don't Remember

As we discover, we remember; remembering, we discover.

—Eudora Welty, *One Writer's Beginnings*

There is so much I don't remember. One minute I was dancing on the polished hardwood floor of the old chapel at the campground on Flathead Lake, where I had performed Rose and Robert's marriage ceremony that morning, and the next minute I was on my hands and knees, using my fingernails to pull myself across the frozen earth toward my cabin. My friend Anna told me later that she woke at 2 A.M. to a high-pitched voice outside moaning, "She's so cold, she's so cold." Wondering where I was, she went out into the dark night to look for me. She found me crumbled in a heap mouthing those words.

I have no memory of making that sound. I seem to recall a strained and disembodied soprano groan at a distance from the right side of my head. But there was no one else there. The left side of my face was smashed in; my shirt and skirt were bloodied and torn. My shoes were missing, and my wire-rimmed glasses were discovered the next day about five hundred yards down the hill toward the lake. The beaded bracelet my parents had given me as an early birthday gift, my fiftieth, was never recovered.

All I know is that two and a half hours of that night are unaccounted for, and the three blankets Anna wrapped around me to warm me next to a roaring fire back in the cabin did nothing to ward off the twenty-four-degree cold I felt in my veins. My "fall" resulted in a severe concussion. Later, the doctor told me I was lucky: I missed breaking my neck by a thread.

Neither my words nor thoughts were sequential for months thereafter, and I would break out in unpredictable sweats fearing that I would never escape the iron diving bell that pressed in on my head. I had explosive angers and uncontrollable tears. The neurologist told me I probably would never recall what happened during the hours I was unconscious in the dark, cold forest. He humored me when I told him I thought I had been swatted by a bear protecting her cub. He thought it was my imagination.

That was seven years ago. He was right; I never recovered the truth of what precipitated my fall. In some ways I know less now than I did then, because at least seven years ago vivid images remained with me. I saw myself flying through the air in slow motion, the shadow of a large tree limb to my left and, nearby, a giant figure that could only have been a bear.

But friends tell me that's impossible, even though bears in every shape and position appeared in the paintings I made for months after the incident. Quite a few flasks of Irish whiskey were passed around that night in the liquor-free campground, so it's not inconceivable that I was drunk. But that's not the image I want to reconstruct. Especially since I had been the minister performing the wedding ceremony for my friends hours before.

So what I am left with is a partial memory. And questions about what has been lost. But that's the thing about memory, isn't it? Memory is rarely whole or factually correct. If the image of the event we have participated in does not match the image of the self we have carefully constructed, then we rarely remember the facts of the event at all. What we remember is a reconstruction of image and feeling that suits our needs and purposes.

The first sense image I have, of flying through the air effortlessly, is filled with surprise and delight. The second image I have, of clawing my way back to the cabin, is accompanied by struggle and pain. What is embedded for me, finally, in the loss of my memory is abject fear.

I recently attended a writing workshop in New York led by poet Myra Shapiro. She asked each of us to write down what we most fear about death. We then traded papers and wrote to someone else's fear. I opened a large piece of lined paper folded into fourths. One of the other women writers had written: "I fear I will not be ready for death."

I wrote in response: "Were you ready for your first kiss, for your first love, for your first penetration? Were you ready for the contractions that swept you into terror and ecstasy giving birth?" I, myself, was not ready for any of these. What I fear most is not death, but living the loss of my life. Awake. Without memory.

My mother died four years ago from complications due to Alzheimer's. Watching the deterioration of first her short-term memory and then her mind terrified me. Chances are my sister, Rosemary, and I could follow her lead down that long dark corridor. That's why the complexities of memory grip me so.

A year after Mom died, Dad sold the house and put everything in storage with A. Fazio Moving and Storage in Ramsey, New Jersey. Dad, Rosemary and I recently unpacked my mother's personal effects from fifty-five years of marriage and eighty-two years of life. The three of us flew to New Jersey to spend a week sorting through thirty huge room-size containers filled with boxes and crates packed with Mom's prized possessions. Dad was now ready to disperse some of Mom's things and had asked Rosemary and me to choose what we wanted. What we each wished for most was a piece of her Waterford crystal or her Rose Medallion china. These, her favorite collections, as well as her rosary beads and stylish hats, most represent our mother to us.

We found several pairs of her rosary beads—crystal, silver and pearl—still inside her bedside table. We discovered the various felt and feathered hats in old-fashioned floral or striped oval hatboxes packed from her closet, but not one piece of crystal or china did we find. My father couldn't remember where he put them after her death—perhaps in storage in Maryland, where he had planned to move to be closer to my sister, or maybe he shipped them to Florida, where he finally decided to reside. When I suggested that we look in storage in Maryland, he said, "No, it's too much trouble."

Two weeks later I dream that I find a dessert dish made of Rose Medallion china; it is a bowl fashioned upon a pedestal, like a goblet. A chalice. It is beautiful and I am pleased in the dream to find this delicate object of exquisite beauty, but some part of my dream-self knows this is a fabrication.

As a young girl of five or six I accompanied my mother to each and every auction or estate sale in New York where she bid for her treasures. I remember a set of early-American Sandwich glass dessert dishes on pedestals that she bought, but there was never a dessert chalice made of Rose Medallion china in her corner closet.

My musings on this dream image bring me to thoughts of memory and memoir: My distorted dream image is like a still photographic exposure capturing a moment in a lifetime. I think about how each genre of collectibles my mother gathered represents a different era in her life. She quit collecting items like the ornate Sandwich glass dessert dishes as she grew in taste and wealth and could afford Waterford crystal; but they reveal her predilection for fine glassware even as she put together our home from estate sales and antique fairs. Her collection of Rose Medallion vases, plates and serving dishes grew as we moved from the community my mother loved, where her friends lived, to a larger home in the country that fit my father's image of himself as his business prospered.

My memory of these collected treasures is clouded by the fact that my mother was unwilling to give any of them to my sister or me before her death or to directly bequeath them to us. A coveted object of desire is thus transformed in my unconscious and becomes a metaphor not only for my mother's fine taste and love of beauty, but also for the manner in which she withheld her love. She was not a woman who easily relinquished what she treasured. This dream chalice of Rose Medallion china becomes a container for both light and dark.

Memory is like that. It is selective; it distorts. It gives pleasure; it reveals disappointment. In her memoir, *Skating to Antarctica,* Jenny Diski writes that we continually create memory from the jigsaw pieces of our experience. But, she cautions us, the stories we tell and retell are utterly unreliable. Who can say whether those jigsaw pieces are actually images from a specific event we remember and not from a photo or movie or some other part of our life? Many people "recall" events from their childhood only from looking at old photo albums. And who can say whether the emotions associated with a particular experience actually belong to it or are simply some feeling we have learned to express?

"Memory is not false in the sense that it is willfully bad," Diski writes, "but it is excitingly corrupt in its inclination to make a proper story of the past." The idea that memory is, in and of itself, "excitingly corrupt," that its function is to make sense of what has happened in a life and to entertain the listener, amuses and intrigues me. That must be why I invented the bear, which brings me to the teller of the memory.

Who is the "I" that remembers? And who tells and retells the story? And how does the voice of the teller change with lived experience and wisdom?

Many years ago my mother gave me two silver bracelets: one, a delicate ring of linked silver leaves she had received from my father, and the other, a large silver and turquoise Indian bracelet from my father's business partner, Art. She asked me not to wear them in front of my father; she did not want him to think she no longer liked the one he had given her, and she gave no response as to why she didn't want him to see the one from Art.

I agreed to comply with her request, but she knew it was inevitable that one day my father would notice the bracelets, because I wore them every day. When he did, he was not offended, but instead told me the story of purchasing the delicate linked-leaf bracelet. "During World War Two, I was stationed in North Carolina learning radio, and while on leave I bought your mother that piece of hammered silver made in Mexico. Notice the craftsmanship; they did such a beautiful job."

Or that is the story I *thought* he told me and the story my mother repeated. That is certainly the story I have told hundreds of times to people admiring the bracelet. This is the memory I recall of the *told* story. When we were packing up the house, however, the bracelet took on a new tale.

"I found that bracelet one day walking up Fifth Avenue in Manhattan," my father said, once again admiring the workmanship on the delicate leaves. "I don't think it was from Tiffany's, because it doesn't look like a Tiffany piece, but I know I bought it on Fifth Avenue."

"But you always told me you bought this for Mom during the war, while you were in training in North Carolina."

"I couldn't have said that. No, that's a piece I found in New York."

Whose memory is correct, and how does each of our particular memories reflect our purpose and identity? Certainly, memory is a reflection of how we see ourselves. The way we tell our life story is the way we begin to live our life.

When my mother gave me the bracelet thirty or more years ago, perhaps I wanted to imagine my father as a bon vivant who found a token of his love for his sweetheart while away at war. Or maybe that's how my mother wanted to remember their early marriage. It was certainly a romantic story for me to hear as a new bride yearning for tokens of my own young husband's love.

But now that my father has retired from his successful advertising career, and my mother has died and he is courting a new love, the story of the bracelet's purchase is associated with another identity—a more prosperous one. The reality is that my mother wore only gold jewelry as they flourished, never silver. She even bleached her beautiful raven-colored mane blond in order to look younger as the wife of a corporate executive. And, as she always told me, blonds wear only gold, never silver.

So I "know" that my father gave my mother that bracelet in the early years of their marriage, when her hair color was brown. And he always said of that time, "We didn't have two pennies to rub together," so he certainly wasn't shopping at a store like Tiffany's on Fifth Avenue in the mid-1940s. So I'm staying with the original story, which is embedded in my memory, no matter what. Does that make my memory excitingly corrupt and my father's conventional, or my memory conventionally romantic and my father's opportunistically corrupt? Or does that just show my stubborn allegiance to my mother's romantic notions about my father and his about himself? What purposes do our differing memories serve?

My memory of the bracelet reflects my feelings about both my mother and my father and my fantasies about their early marriage. Of course, these fantasies were influenced by the movies about World War II romances I watched when we first had a television set in the mid-fifties. So my memory is a mixture of images and desires: photographs of my mother in her late twenties with raven-colored hair, waiting for her husband to return from the war; movies with stars like Myrna Loy also awaiting their loved one's return from a movie war; my mother's longing for a simple marriage; my desire to create harmony between what I wanted for my mother and my father's mythology about himself, right out of a Horatio Alger story.

So perhaps memory in a pure, virginal, untainted state can never exist and Jenny Diski is right. Perhaps memory is more than excitingly corrupt; perhaps it is purely invention, a particular point of view, an angle of perception. A created fiction. Perhaps it is the nature of memory to glow with contamination. And if the memoirist is a self-conscious cultivator of his or her own myth, then it is even more difficult to separate fact from fiction.

In her essay in *The Anatomy of Memory,* Toni Morrison writes that the deliberate act of remembering is a form of willed creation. Few of us aside from historians try to find out what actually happened during a particular event, because, quite frankly, we don't have time or the desire to research. We dwell instead on the way the event appeared to us and why it appeared in that particular way. My bear probably appeared because it resembled the shadows of the trees on that barely moonlit night and fit well with my mythology about the land and bear spirits.

Memory therefore is a way of creating one's identity. And that is exactly what a memoirist does when she chooses a particular memory for illumination—she recreates her sense of identity. The memoirist takes a slice of life, a remembered image, and chews on it, munching slowly if not perhaps deliberately, to extract as much nutrition—as much meaning—from it as possible. She does more than relive the experience; she tries to make sense of the relationship between the remembered image and the feelings contained in the image that have caused her to safely store it away for later review.

We know that we usually remember images that carry strong feelings. Powerful emotions, positive or negative, are vivid. The feelings I associate with my free fall through the Montana night air are vaguely pleasurable; in fact, they override my memory of extreme cold when I hit the ground. I can easily conjure up the lightness of my being, but I don't want to feel the icy chill of my limp limbs. The passage of time and my fear of recovering what has been lost have forced my feelings associated with the memory and the stored image to become estranged. Writing memoir heals that estrangement.

The job of writing memoir is to find one's truth, not to determine the accuracy of what happened; that is history, a testimony, perhaps even an interesting tale. The memoirist, instead, both recounts an event and muses upon it. What meaning, what value do I attach to how my life has unfolded? How did this happen, how did that happen? Not *why* did this happen; that is explored in psychotherapy, which is not my focus here. However, finding out the truth of what happened can certainly challenge one's sense of self.

To find out how an event happened, we have to look at the *details* of our life, and those details come through the sensory images we have stored. We go back in time and see, smell, taste, feel or hear a particular scene, and we begin to appreciate the richness and idiosyncrasy of our unique existence. But because these events are not happening in present time, we have to use our imagination to reclaim them. So we can never separate the remembered event from our imagination: They stick together.

I am five years old, sitting at my father's drafting table in the basement of our unfinished family room in Hohokus, New Jersey. I am looking up through a transom window at the light flickering through the windblown leaves of a tree at ground level in our backyard, trying to figure out how to draw the branches growing from out of the trunk of the tree.

My father has lent me his Prismacolor pencils, and I am thrilled by the variety of greens that I can use for the leaves. There are so many more colors in this box of pencils than there are in my box of thick Crayola crayons at school. And with those, I always have to stay within the lines.

My father is somewhere nearby working on a project, perhaps measuring out how much wooden paneling he will need to buy for the walls of the basement. I don't remember what he is actually doing; that detail seems irrelevant to my memory of the event. I just know that he is working close by and that I want to learn how to draw a tree, and I assume he knows how to draw one because he's an artist. Therefore, I want him to teach me.

"Daddy, will you teach me how to draw a tree?"

"Just look at the tree and draw it."

"I'm looking at the tree, but I can't get the branches to come out right. They look like they're hugging each other in real life, and I can't make them hug on paper."

"Just keep looking at the tree and put down what you see."

"I am, but it doesn't look right."

"Well, you either have it or you don't."

Did he really say that, or was that my imagination? Did I make that up? Could an artist father really say that to his five-year-old daughter about drawing a *tree*? "You either have it or you don't"? No, I didn't believe it either.

But why would I make that up? I actually had a hard time believing my five-year-old memory, even though I could still feel the sting of his words, until I met Wallis, a writer friend from Italy who recounted a similar experience that she had with her artist father in the Midwest, in the 1950s. He wasn't even a New Yorker! He too said, "You either have it or you don't."

I remember the sound of my father's words—he didn't even look up at me when he said them—and I remember how I felt: ashamed. My face got red. I put my pencil down, closed his box of Prismacolor pencils, climbed down from his chair at the drafting table and trudged up the open stairs to the kitchen. I stopped drawing. Now remember, I was five years old and I believed my father. He knew; he was an artist, he worked with artists, and he said you either have it or you don't. And I couldn't make the trees look the way I saw them no matter how long and carefully I looked at them, so I didn't "have" it. Whatever the "it" was that artists had.

Now, in retrospect, I know that part of me shut down that day. I stopped seeing the colors dance in the trees, glimmer like rainbows in the ice on the pond and sing in the waterfall. Up until that day, color had made me happy; it flirted and glowed, it felt like a warm towel after a bath, it gave me chills like my neighbor's puppy licking my face, it sang. Something about color comforted me.

I was very sad that night. Sad that I didn't have it. Sad that "it" was something I didn't know how to get. Sad that "it" was finite. No, I didn't know that word when I was five, but I felt that feeling. "It" felt limited. I'd have to find a way to get "it," but I was afraid I wouldn't be able to.

I started to walk to Mass every day to pray for "it," and the feelings I began to develop at Mass—the stirrings that accompanied the ritual, the incense, the candles and the statue of Mary that moved if I stared at her long enough in the candlelight—got mixed up with my yearnings to be an artist. I decided that since I couldn't draw trees and be like my daddy, I would become a nun. I could *do* that. And it would make my mommy happy. And I didn't think you had to have "it" to become holy.

I tell this memory not to portray my father as an arrogant monster (although when younger, I wanted to) or to sound like a whining child (although I have no control over what you may think of me), but because of the symbolic nature, the *meaning* I attached to that particular memory, certainly unconsciously at the time the event occurred, and more consciously as I have come to understand my own interpretation of the events.

The details of the memory—the tree viewed through the transom, the green and brown Prismacolor pencils marked by my baby teeth, my father's drafting table with my unfinished drawing left on it and my feelings of loss—all became symbolic of my lifelong struggle to get my father to take me seriously, to overcome my feelings of not having what it takes to be a certain type of artist and to enjoy my own brand of creativity.

The details of our memories are important: They are not mere information or flat facts. They help us recognize the symbolic nature of the event. The impression my baby teeth made on my father's colored pencils is a small detail, yes, but it reveals to me just how determined I was to learn how to draw.

The meaning of the event is not attached to the details, but details help disclose the meaning of the event. What is important about memoir is the meaning we make of our lives, and of course, that meaning is subjective. Flying through the air, clawing my way across the frozen earth, the disembodied voice intoning "She's so cold," and the swat of the bear's paw—those are details that I remember of that night at Flathead Lake. The meaning I made of those details changed my life forever. I stopped performing marriage ceremonies for four years after that incident, because I felt that I was not in harmony with myself. My own marriage ended before the year was over.

So the details are more important than we give them credit for. They not only lend credence to the validity of the story and perhaps make the writing of a memoir more layered; they also help reveal the emotions embedded in the images we recount. We gather the jigsaw pieces of our experience and put them together in a story we tell and retell until we get the memory right.

Jigsaw Pieces of Memory

I am forced to admit that memory is not a warehouse of finished stories,
not a gallery of framed pictures. I must admit that I invented.
—Patricia Hampl, *I Could Tell You Stories*

My mother was a demanding yet beautiful woman. She was always impeccably dressed, her hair carefully coifed, and she never left the house, even to buy a quart of milk, without wearing lipstick and her girdle. She wore veiled pillbox hats before Jackie Kennedy made them fashionable and blue-and-white spectator shoes perfectly polished the first day of spring. She attended daily Mass at our local church, taught me how to dance the Charleston in our basement and let me lick the leftover batter in the bowl when she made chocolate cakes. She also had frequent, debilitating headaches.

When I was about seven years old I learned how to make hot compresses. My mother would lie on her bed with the drapes pulled shut and call my name. I knew what she wanted when I walked into the darkened room. I would go into her bathroom, take one of her freshly washed white face cloths, fold it into thirds lengthwise and turn on the tap until steam rose from the faucet. As the hot water washed over the terry cloth, I would poke it with my index finger to see if it was hot enough. When it was as hot as I could stand it, I squeezed the water out of the face cloth and laid it across my mother's forehead and sinuses. I made a game of seeing how hot I could make the compress; my mother seemed pleased when it was boiling hot. When the compress cooled, I repeated the process.

In between trips to the sink, I looked at the objects on my mother's vanity table: her silver-handled hairbrush and beveled hand mirror, her black enamel capsules of red, red lipstick, the elegantly shaped glass perfume bottles. Sometimes, when her mood wasn't too dark, she would let me dab her Chanel No. 5 behind my ear. I loved the smell that escaped from the bottle when I removed the glass stopper and the sensation of the rich balm on my neck.

I tell this story because my memory of this childhood experience resides in my fingertips. I can almost feel the heat from the compress in my hands, and that sense memory leads me to yet another: massaging my mother's back as she aged.

As my mother's illness progressed and her memory deteriorated, the part of her identity she most fiercely clung to was her girdle. Like most women of her generation, she wore a girdle every day; no outfit was complete without what she and her friends called their "foundation." When her health failed, she refused to remove her girdle; she wore it day and night, whether awake or asleep. She was determined to wear it even when I tried to give her a massage several months before her death.

"Mom, take off your girdle so I can massage your lower back." She ignores me as she climbs onto the bed after removing her blouse and bra and tossing them onto a chair. This action surprises me because my mother has never before allowed me to see her even partially naked. Women didn't do that in the fifties. I pull the top sheet over her lower body and nudge her gently to the middle of the bed so I can sit down beside her.

"I'm going to put some oil on your back, Mom. Is that okay?"

"Whatever you say, dear."

I enjoy massaging my mother's back, because she was never a woman who welcomed touch and I am grateful that she allows it now. There's also never been a time before in my life when my mother said, "Whatever you say, dear." Not to me, not to my father, not to my younger sister. No, my mother argued about whether it was night or day. She was a rigid perfectionist with a code of order in which things were either black or white; she brooked no gray. We took off our shoes when we came in the back door; tracking mud into the kitchen could result in plates flung crashing to the floor. The dulcet tones of this woman calling me "dear" are an anomaly. Who is this imposter, this sweet, acquiescent aging woman? For the first time in my life, I'd like the sharp-tongued firebrand back.

I start to massage her left shoulder and rub oil down the length of her spine. I'm immediately struck by how small she has become. I massaged this same back the year before, when she had fallen in the kitchen, incurring a concussion. But it wasn't the same back then. Then, it was swollen and bruised. Then, she let me pull down her ever-present girdle. But not now.

"I have to have my girdle," she says as I try to coax her to take it off. "I can't do without it."

"Why, Mom? Why now?"

"You know I always wore a girdle. I need it."

"But I can't rub your lower back with your girdle on."

Silence. The girdle remains. I surrender.

My mother remembered her girdle as part of her identity. Her sense memory retained the scaffolding of her disposition.

One of the hallmarks of memoir writing is its intimacy with its audience. In writing this vignette, my intent is not to humiliate my mother, but to show her determination. My mother's refusal to take off her girdle was a metaphor for her desperate attempt to maintain some control over her life even as she was losing her mind. The fact that it was such a losing battle made her defiance even more poignant and my inability to alleviate her suffering even more final.

Not long after my mother died, I read John Bayley's memoir *Elegy for Iris,* about his wife, Iris Murdoch, and her struggle with Alzheimer's. Bayley's description of the nightly "trouser wars," during which he could not get his wife to relinquish her trousers, helped me understand my mother's ritualistic attachment to her girdle. No doctor could explain my mother's behavior to me, but writing my account of the girdle wars and reading Bayley's memoir made its meaning clear. Both helped me sort out the puzzle pieces of our relationship.

In writing about my mother, I am trying to put her back together by passing her on to the future in the only way I can—as memory. When I write about her and the complexity of our relationship, I try to bring her alive in the most honest way I can—for a moment. This moment. In another moment, I might write something quite different.

Essayist Michael Ventura wrote that Henry Miller was fond of quoting his friend Fred Perlès: "'The mission of man on earth is to remember.' To re-member. To put back together. To re-attach a lost member." The idea of reattaching a lost member of our tribe through memory is a remarkable concept, because, in truth, that may be the most tangible experience we have of one another. Memories are particular and fragmented, and they are all we have to offer the loved ones with whom we have shared life. That's what we do when we write memoir: We put back together fragments of our life and the lives of our loved ones in a way that reflects the universal experience of being human. In doing so, we become a part of each other.

Memory and Truth

How do we know, when we write a memoir, whether we have told the truth of our reminiscence or embellished it with our imagination? We probably don't, at least not in the first draft. All we can ask of ourselves as we struggle to reconstruct our memory is that we give the reader the best of our recollection.

Author Mary McCarthy writes about the vagaries of memory in her preface to *Memories of a Catholic Girlhood*. She wonders whether some of the incidents that she recalls from her childhood actually happened or whether she made them up. Her parents died when she was very young, so the chain of recollection, the collective memory of her family, was broken. She and her siblings were farmed out to various extended family members, so she had no one to correct her recollections—or to say, "That couldn't have happened the way you remember it, that's impossible."

She gives the hilarious example of her son, Reuel, who at one time was convinced that Mussolini had been thrown off a bus in North Truro on Cape Cod, during the Second World War. This memory goes back to one morning in 1943 when, as a young child, he was waiting with his mother and father beside the road in Wellfleet to put a departing guest on the bus to Hyannis. The bus came through and the bus driver leaned down to shout the latest piece of news: "They've thrown Mussolini out!"

As an adult, Reuel now knows that Mussolini was never ejected from a Massachusetts bus, and he knows where he got that impression. But if McCarthy and her husband had died that year, their son would have been left with a clear recollection of something that everyone would have assured him was a historical impossibility, with no way of reconciling his stubborn memory to the stubborn facts on record. His "memory" would have been wrong.

Memory, through imagination, can impose a value beyond that of the actual experience. The value or meaning of the experience may be lost with the passage of time, but some trace of the feeling associated with it still exists. Whether it's a feeling of joy about the delightful innocence of childhood, anger over a perceived injustice, longing for an unrequited love, or grief and powerlessness over the loss of a loved one, the feeling lives somewhere deep within us. I still feel sadness about being unable to alleviate my mother's fear and anxiety as she approached the end of her life, even though I know there was nothing more I could do. When she repeatedly said, "Something is very wrong," I could soothe her in the moment, but I couldn't take away her underlying fear, because at some level we both knew it was true.

Memoir and Myth

I have always been fascinated by myth—it must come in the holy water when you grow up Irish and are baptized Catholic. My father has always been a great teller of tales, particularly when it comes to his own embellished exploits, and the chief reading my mother kept around the house was *The Lives of the Saints*. So I was raised on harrowing tales told to me about twelve-year-old virgin martyrs like Maria Goretti, stabbed to death by a rejected suitor, and Lucia, who had her throat slit for the same reason and was forever immortalized holding her two eyes in a dish. The male saints seemed to survive adolescence somewhat better, so I switched my allegiance to Francis of Assisi, who developed the gift of gab with animals while wandering the countryside, begging for food. These early stories became my childhood myths.

In the 1980s, I became intrigued by the popularity of Bill Moyers's series *Joseph Campbell and the Power of Myth*. I had worked and studied with Campbell during the late seventies and early eighties when he taught in California, and like many other Campbellites, I was captivated by his ability to weave together stories, languages and images from each and every culture and find a common thread. His understanding of the continuing power of myth in modern life offered me a new way to look at the repeating patterns lived out in each generation. He challenged all of us to live our lives as if, in his words, "You were what you really are." His work touched a nerve for me about finding meaning.

I write about Campbell and the power of myth because inherent in both myth and memoir is a search for meaning. Memoir, like mythology, shares a depth of inquiry. Both myth and memoir examine the important questions in life: Who am I? Who do I belong to? What is my tribe? Where am I going? How do I make my way? What is my purpose? Whether our distant ancestors looked to the sun, moon and stars for guidance and direction or our contemporary relations pin their hopes and dreams on meditation, organized religion, the stock market or biotechnology, we have always, as a species, yearned for meaning.

Myth owes its longevity to its power to express typical human emotions that have been experienced throughout successive generations. Memoir owes its popularity to its ability to portray these same enduring feelings in a contemporary individual's life. Both myth and memoir arose from a human need for connection. Myths use symbols and gods and goddesses to explore such themes as heroism, betrayal, the search for the mother or the father, love and the cycles of death and rebirth. Memoirs explore the very same themes in the stories of everyday lives. Memoirists are our contemporary mythmakers.

Three summers ago, while on an early morning walk though the hay fields outside Lavigny, Switzerland, I met a woman walking her dog. We fell into step next to each other and she asked me if I was staying at the writers' residency. When I told her yes, she asked me what I was writing. I tentatively mumbled something about memory and metaphor, hoping she wouldn't pursue the conversation. It's hard for me to discuss what I'm writing about when I'm in the middle of it. Instead, she immediately asked, "Do you know Joseph Campbell?" When I said yes, she told me that her friends had sent her the tapes of his interviews with Moyers years ago when she had lived in India working as an economist. In the three weeks I had been writing in Lavigny, no one had ever spoken to me on my early morning forays in the fields, and here I was, at 7 A.M., discussing mythology with a Swiss economist from Bern who had learned about the power of myth while working in India!

Because we have become such a mobile culture, living, in many cases, across continents from our families and loved ones, we yearn for community, consciously or not. Reading a memoir or sitting in a memoir class listening to the lives of other people gives us a sense of perspective about our own life as well as a link to a community. If I write about some experience in my life and reflect on it in such a way that it touches your experience of your life, then we have made a connection, regardless of our difference in class, ethnicity or gender. We may not be aware of it at the time, but something happens on a deep level to both of us.

When I first read *Daughter of the Queen of Sheba,* Jacki Lyden's memoir about growing up with a manic depressive mother, I had a very visceral response. Lyden longed to know what was going on inside her mother's mind when she was lost to a manic episode; I longed to know what was going on inside my mother's mind as she was lost to memory. I thought of the ancient Greek myth about Demeter's search for her daughter, Persephone, who was abducted into the underworld by Hades. Anyone who has experienced madness in a parent, child, lover or oneself knows how similar it is to an abduction into the underworld. The loved one is lost to all who love her, including herself.

Lyden is a senior correspondent for National Public Radio and an expert on the Middle East; she covered both the Gulf War and the Afghan War. In her poignant memoir about trying to find her mother in one of her manic episodes, she writes:

> I longed to know my mother's secret language when she went mad. I yearned to know its passwords and frames of reference. In the last and most desperate stages of mania, my mother's speech falls to pure sound. . . . I have become obsessed with finding her in a chiaroscuro world where, despite every art of intimacy that I have ever learned, I am in high seas. She is lost. And I cannot follow.

Demeter could have said the same thing about her lost daughter Persephone, carted off by Hades to the underworld. Demeter could not follow. She could rant, she could rave, she could make demands upon Zeus for her daughter's return, she could strike terror in the hearts of mankind by causing famine, but she could not follow. Persephone had to make her own way out, and both suffered the consequences.

I too could not follow my mother as each neuron in her cortex withered and she looked at me in panic and said, "What's happening? I think I'm losing my mind. Help me." I could rant, I could cry, I could curse my mother's doctor. I could pray to a god I no longer believed was merciful. But I could not follow. The pre-Christian corn goddess Demeter, war correspondent Lyden and I all share the same mythic dilemma: powerlessness in the face of a loved one's abduction and loss.

In every society mythmakers start with an archetype, which can be understood as an invisible primary pattern, such as the mother-child bond, which we cannot actually perceive but whose energy propels us. Lyden yearns for her mother much like Persephone must have longed for her mother, whom she could no longer reach. The mythmaker creates a specific story that expresses the invisible pattern: in this case, mother-daughter loss. But the mythmaker is inventing only the current manifestation of a mythic theme that already exists unconsciously in the collective.

For example, in ancient literature, Odysseus's journey across the seas was invented or appropriated to serve as a Greek expression of heroism, and in the twentieth-century cultural lexicon of film, Luke Skywalker's journey in the skies was invented to serve as a Western expression of heroism. Both heroes represent something of our own psychological journey. The myth of Odysseus is passed on from generation to generation by acculturation, but the hero archetype is passed on through constantly repeated experiences of human existence.

Myth is a way of seeing through things. If myths are to help us question and go deeper, we must move to a place of neither belief nor disbelief, but a place of make-believe. The language of poetry, art, theater and music exist because the ultimate core of meaning may be depicted but not directly described. Myth, too, circumscribes and gives an approximate description of an unconscious core of meaning. The memoir also tries to frame a particular slice of life in order to make sense of it. In reflecting on the purpose of memoir, Lyden writes:

We have survived, we are at the end of our journey, we want to, like Odysseus, make some sense of where we have gone. . . . That means we must have digested the experience, not merely confessed it. We must have a little compassion for the selves that we are delving into here, not a sense of revenge or self-pity.

This is one of the reasons for the current popularity of memoir; we all search for a way to express our lives and we yearn for an experience of the commonality of our human existence. The extraordinary response to Frank McCourt's memoir, *Angela's Ashes,* illustrates the human need for each life to be seen and heard. McCourt's memoir of growing up in poverty in the Limerick slums with an alcoholic father on the dole and a mother who grieves each baby's death from starvation describes a universal experience rarely articulated with such grace and humor. In a sense his tale is mythic, because it demonstrates the heroism and dignity of the human spirit. It stirs our collective memory and inspires our collective compassion.

Perhaps a few writers use memoir as little more than an exercise in narcissism, but they are the exception. True memoir, that which struggles with insight and self-reflection, demonstrates a yearning to connect with the whole world. In the act of remembering, we expand beyond ourselves.

Memory in Transit

The memory is a living thing—it too is in transit.

—Eudora Welty, *One Writer's Beginnings*

I watched helplessly one day as my mother tried to set the lunch table for my son, his girlfriend, my father, herself and me. She looked at us and took three knives out of the drawer. I waited to see if she would take more. She put them on the table together and picked up the napkins. She walked back to the drawer and took out three spoons. She looked at all of us and counted. "One . . . two . . . three . . . four . . . five."

"Mom, let's get two more," I said as I handed her two additional knives and spoons. She tried to match each spoon with each knife, but the more she tried, the more this simple task eluded her. Her frustration grew as she attempted to make sense of what I can only imagine must have been a chaos of shapes. Abruptly, she threw everything down on the table. She looked at me in terror and mumbled, "I just can't do it," and rushed out the kitchen door.

My heart sank. In that moment, I felt what it must be like to know you are not who you once knew yourself to be, to understand that your loss of memory has completely changed your identity. She declined more rapidly after this incident.

Our identity is always in flux; our present identity alters the past even as our past identity informs our present. But the deliberate act of remembering is always a form of willed creation—an intentional creating of identity. Once a person's will is stolen by an illness such as depression or Alzheimer's disease, her memory is muted. Therefore, in losing memory we conceivably lose our sense of self. People with a strong sense of identity have the most difficulty coping with Alzheimer's. As they lose their ability to concentrate and to form coherent sentences, they cannot share with others what they still formulate in their minds.

In *Elegy for Iris,* Bayley wonders about his wife: "Does Iris speak, inside herself, of what is happening? How can I know? What is left is the terrible expectancy. 'When?' and 'I want.' Is she still saying inside herself, like the blind man in Faulkner's *Soldiers' Pay*: 'When are they going to let me out?'"

My mother's Alzheimer's lament was "When am I going home?" When she could still dress herself, she would put on the same black-and-white houndstooth skirt and white blouse every day and stand at the front door, inside the vestibule of my parents' house and anxiously ask:

"Am I going home today?"

"Mom, you are home."

"No, am I going home today?"

"You are home, Mom. This is your home."

"When am I going home?"

It would break my father's heart to hear her repeatedly ask to go home, and sometimes he would help her into the car, drive around the block or to the local hot dog stand and then bring her back again. "We're home, Julia," he would say enthusiastically as he pulled up to the front door and helped her out of the car. And she would smile and go inside and say it all over again.

The most jolting indication of my mother's loss of identity came the day she and my father walked down the driveway to the white wrought-iron mailbox in front of their house and she asked him to read the name plate on the box. "Are we Hennesseys?" she asked after he read their name. "Yes, sweetheart, you've been a Hennessey for a long time. Fifty-five years."

"Oh," she said, "I didn't know." They walked back inside, she to their bedroom, he to the kitchen, where he sat down and cried. After that day, she called him "Mr. Hennessey" until the only word she could say was his first name, "Matt."

Bayley felt that his wife's lack of a strong sense of identification with being a writer made it easier for her to float into the world of preoccupied emptiness experienced by Alzheimer's patients. As her illness progressed, Iris had no memory of the fact that she had written twenty-six novels, as well as books on philosophy, and had become a Dame of the British Empire. However, when an admirer or friend would ask her to sign a copy of one of her books, surprised at first by the request, she would comply by laboriously writing her name and, if she could, theirs.

"It takes her some time," Bayley writes, "but the letters are still formed with care, and resemble, in a surreal way, her old handwriting. She is always anxious to oblige. And the old gentleness remains."

These two women's loss of identity strikes me as a metaphor for the lost stories of my mother's generation. So many of my contemporaries know almost nothing about the inner lives of the women who gave birth to them, outside of their experience of them as mothers. Yes, we may know something of their work life, their preferences in fashion or food, what values they espoused and passed on to us, but we know little about their secret longings, their frustrated ambitions, their unlived loves.

I know that my mother worked in insurance before the Second World War, that her preference in food tended toward Italian, that her first love, Brian Murphy, became a priest like her brother, and that she always wanted to run an antiques store of her own. Like many women of her generation, she was expected to relinquish her job when the men came home from the war, return home, make babies and take care of the family. Her dream of an antiques shop was never realized, and the details of her inner life remained hidden.

I surmised that my father was not her first love only because my mother blushed like a schoolgirl every time Father Murphy came to visit. After one of his visits, I said, "Rosemary and I would have had red hair if you had married Father Murphy, Mom," but she just smiled and remained silent. Details of their courtship were never forthcoming, only her feeling of loss.

Women of my mother's generation didn't tell such stories, and they certainly didn't write them down. I know that they may have talked to each other about their children and their frustrations with their husbands, but they had neither the time nor the permission to examine their lives. Women speaking their truth was taboo; convention, polite society and the Church did not allow it.

One day my mother came home crying: Her friend Peggy had taken her life. The word "suicide" was never spoken; in fact, my mother never told me anything about what had happened to my friend Kevin's mom. The next day at school I heard that she "had taken too many pills," but when I asked my mother about what I had heard, she would only say, "Peggy had a problem."

I didn't know that Peggy was an alcoholic who was driven to despair by tranquilizers and too many responsibilities. It was not respectable to speak of such desperation in the late fifties. In fact, it was considered a mortal sin to take one's life, and a mortal sin was much too dark to discuss. So my mother never spoke about what Peggy had suffered. I kept wondering what could have been so bad for her to leave her children and subject herself to an eternity in Hell. But the next thing we knew, Kevin and his brothers and sister had a stepmother. Soon, no one in our neighborhood spoke of Peggy. Her story remained untold.

If we never learn our mothers' memories and their stories, we are helpless to make the future—for ourselves and our daughters. In the silencing of our mothers' lives and our own, we lose identity. It has been a gradual process for women to discover their voice. It took the momentum of the women's movement of the early seventies for women to feel they had a right to their own identity and collectively to speak their truth.

Women's Memoirs

In 1973, American poet and novelist May Sarton gave women

permission to speak their truth. This was the year she wrote her memoir *Journal of a Solitude*. Her previous book, *Plant Dreaming Deep,* published five years earlier, was an extraordinary and beautiful account of her adventure in buying a house in New England and living alone.

In *Writing a Woman's Life,* Carolyn Heilbrun recounts that *Plant Dreaming Deep* eventually disappointed Sarton, "as she came to realize that none of the anger, passionate struggle, or despair of her life was revealed in her writing. She had not intentionally concealed her pain; she had written in the old genre of female autobiography, which tends to find beauty even in pain and to transform rage into spiritual acceptance."

Later, as she read her idealized life in the letters she received from readers seeking to emulate her, she realized that in ignoring her rage and pain she had unintentionally been dishonest. The change in women's consciousness in the 1970s helped bring her to this realization. In *Journal of a Solitude,* she deliberately set out to recount the pain of the years covered in *Plant Dreaming Deep* by naming her anger and depression, even though it was still unacceptable for a woman to openly express either her angst or her desire to live her own life:

> We go up to Heaven and down to Hell a dozen times a day—at least, I do. And the discipline of work provides an exercise bar, so that the wild, irrational motions of the soul become formal and creative. It literally keeps one from falling on one's face.

Sarton's honesty made it acceptable for women to write about their true feelings. Her courage opened up the genre of memoir writing for women; they were able to name their independent lives.

In her study of autobiography, *When Memory Speaks,* Jill Ker Conway, a memoirist and academic, takes a historical look at the differences between male and female autobiography. She discovers that the biggest difference between men's and women's memoirs lies in *agency*: whether the narrator is the agent of her own life and celebrates her triumphs and failures, or whether the narrator lives in reaction to forces around her.

According to Conway, male autobiography has typically taken the form of the mythic hero based on the Greek ideal of heroism. Life for a man is a quest filled with trials and obstacles, which he must surmount alone through courage, cunning and moral strength. Eventually, unless the hero has displeased the gods, he achieves his goal. Whether this goal is money, political power, rescuing an abducted wife, scaling a mountain or acquiring spiritual knowledge, he survives his journey and returns home to claim his rightful place in the world. His achievement comes through his own agency.

In contrast, the earliest recorded women's memoirs, such as those by the twelfth-century German abbess Hildegard of Bingen, fourteenth-century British religious Dame Julian of Norwich and Teresa of Avila, a sixteenth-century Spanish mystic, are personal accounts of each writer's relationship with God. In these, each woman records her inner life devoted to an intense and visionary contact with God, which requires a surrender of personal will. As a result of Saint Paul's influence on Christian scripture, women in the Church were expected to remain silent. Secular women in post-Renaissance Europe were left out of democratic debate and were denied a voice in matters of either politics or theology. They were not allowed to develop a sense of independent agency; they either served God, their fathers or their husbands.

Conway discovered that nineteenth-century women's autobiographies were by and large preoccupied with the quest for the ideal mate, who owned property and had social mobility. This quest relied on a woman's emotional response and what happened *to* her—in relationship to her lovers or reversals of fortune—not her independent agency. At the turn of the twentieth century, many stories of women's struggles for education and equality—the vote, birth control and social work—could have been seen as heroic, but since these women did not make or control great fortunes like Carnegie and Rockefeller, their power remained unacknowledged. Instead, their competence and authority was shrouded in service and self-sacrifice. Their success was not attributed to any sense of personal agency—it "just happened." Unless their lives were linked to the histories of famous men, women who did write about their lives addressed their interior lives rather than their actions in the world.

One of Conway's discoveries had a great impact on me: Because, historically, women haven't felt entitled to a private destiny, they feel conflict between their sense of a true vocation and their sense of duty to family. That was certainly true for me in my early twenties. I did not feel entitled to shape my own future; that was not a concept I had learned from my mother's life.

I barely gave a second thought to declining a full National

Institute of Mental Health fellowship to attend graduate school in order to stay home and care for my first child. Although I was very proud to receive the award and disappointed not to be able to pursue my own graduate studies, it was not a point of lengthy discussion between my husband and me. He had not been accepted at the law school where I had received the fellowship to graduate school. In spite of the inroads the women's movement was starting to make in the late sixties, it had not yet touched us. My husband's legal studies and the care of our son came first.

Conway writes that it takes only one free choice to change the outcome of a person's life. She left the outback of Australia to study in the United States and eventually became the president of Smith College. In her memoir *The Road from Cooraⁱn,* she writes about developing her strong independent identity through access to education. She also tells the story of her difficulty separating from her mother, who was such a strong presence in her psyche that she felt if she did not separate from her, she would die.

For many a woman, the forging of a strong independent identity does not occur until she leaves home. The bond she has with her mother (or her idealization of her father) is so strong that it takes years for her to differentiate herself from her family identity. Conway had to put enormous geographical distance between her mother and herself to create her own life.

I left home for college at seventeen, but I didn't really extricate myself from my mother's web until I married and had a child. And that was not a conscious choice; in many ways, my first free choice occurred one day in confession a year after my first child was born.

I had gone to confession, as we still did in the late sixties, on a

Saturday afternoon. At the time, my husband was a second-year law student; I was home caring for my ten-month-old son, who had just stopped nursing. I had just started to use birth control. Kneeling in the dark confessional, I "confessed" to the priest that I was using birth control, assuming he would tell me to say ten Hail Marys, absolve me, and that would be that. But instead he told me he could not grant me pardon unless I stopped using birth control. I was incredulous.

"You can't absolve me? What does that mean, Father, you can't absolve me?"

"You can't receive the sacraments until you stop using birth control. Have you tried nursing your child?"

"Yes, Father, I have. My baby just stopped nursing. And nursing doesn't guarantee that a woman won't get pregnant; that's an old wives' tale. My husband is in law school and we can't afford to have another baby, because I'm only working part-time. We have to use birth control."

"Well, I can't absolve you unless you tell me that you are not going to use birth control."

"Are you asking me to lie?"

"No. I'm asking you to tell me that you will not use birth control."

"But I just told you that I will. You're asking me to purposefully tell you a lie."

I got up and left the confessional confused and shaken. Immediately I heard the priest open his door behind me. He was young, probably only a couple of years older than me. He was also clearly shaken. "Come back," he said, "let's work something out."

"But you want me to pretend that I won't do something that

I told you I'm going to do," I said. "I can't lie just so you can absolve me."

There was nothing more for either of us to say. I left the church and walked home. I was outraged and deeply saddened that there was no room for compassion in the faith that I had practiced for twenty-two years. In many ways, that was my first experience of self-agency in an area that had so structured and nurtured my identity. I was devastated.

Until the women's movement in the seventies, women allowed a lot to "happen" to them, or they acquiesced to cultural expectations, religious norms and the benefits of family roles. Creating a sense of independent identity brings with it a great deal of responsibility and vulnerability. I don't think many women of my generation thought much about self-agency until Betty Friedan wrote *The Feminine Mystique*. Yes, we might have performed small acts of rebellion against parents, teachers and others in authority, but it wasn't until the early seventies that women started to make more conscious decisions about how to construct their lives. Many of the changes brought about by the women's movement have been extremely painful and have altered the fabric of society; transformation at this level of women's personal and global agency does not occur without a price.

Memoir has given women the freedom to write about what it means not only to be a woman shaped by the values of contemporary society, but to be a woman shaping the values of contemporary society: how she sees her position in the world, what her role is in her family and how she balances the needs of others with the call of her own destiny. Women's memoir also probes the longings, moral decisions, defiance, suffering, pain and triumphs of the human soul. Many current women's memoirs deal with issues that society has left unexamined knowing that these issues exist in the abstract but preferring to ignore the specifics: race, class, father-daughter incest, alcoholism, Alzheimer's, religious oppression, the deterioration of the family, harassment in the workplace, environmental destruction. In recalling their experience of these issues, women are forging their own identity and redefining public discourse.

The Voice of the Memoirist

The voice the memoirist selects determines to a large extent her identity. The narrator does not simply describe events in her life; she selects what events to tell and shares her insights about them. How she tells the story—rather than what the events are—allows the reader to discover what it is the writer wants to find out about herself as well as what she wants the reader to know. Many women memoirists write passionately about what they come to understand about themselves and their society. A case in point is Terry Tempest Williams's *Leap,* a memoir about her deep exploration of questions that grew out of her relationship with a painting.

Williams is a poet, a Mormon and an environmentalist who lives in Utah. She grew up with a print of Hieronymus Van Acken Bosch's *El Jardín de las Delícias* hanging on the bulletin board above the bed in which she slept while visiting her grandmother's house. The print was a diptych from the Metropolitan Museum of Art that displayed two panels: the Garden of Eden, with Christ taking Eve's pulse as Adam looks on, opposite an image of Hell. As a child, Williams loved looking at it as she and her siblings fell asleep beneath Truth and Evil. It wasn't until she went to the Prado in Spain as an adult that she saw the complete painting for the first time. It is actually a triptych that includes a center panel, the Garden of Earthly Delights.

What had been kept from Williams's view was the celebration of naked bodies cavorting with Eros. The realization that this reflection of her own body had been hidden from her during her childhood was deeply disturbing. It provoked a period of internal questioning that changed her life profoundly. Over the next several years, she traveled periodically to Spain to sit with the painting in the Prado and explore the connections between Bosch's fifteenth-century vision and her own life. In the process of writing her memoir, Williams examined issues regarding her faith, her marriage, her ancestry and the environment. She came to terms with her deep commitment to them all:

> Inside my veins, I feel the pulse of my people, those dead and those standing beside me, a pulse I will always be driven by, a pulse that registers as a murmur in my heart. I cannot escape my history, nor can I ignore the lineage that is mine. Most importantly, I don't want to.

Williams's poetic prose gives voice to the memory of her lineage and the element of free choice that allows her to return to the faith of her ancestors. Inspiration from Bosch's vision helps her recognize that the past and future are contemporary. In her brilliant exploration, she gently challenges the reader to examine her own life as well.

I pull myself into a ball in the bathtub deep in the hot water, trying to get warm after three days of rain, thinking about Williams's words: "How can we learn to speak in a language that is *authentic,* faithful to our hearts?" Williams has made speaking and writing authentically a practice, much like one of the precepts of Buddhism. She challenges each one of us to do the same. I muse on the difference, in writing memoir, between authenticity and a reactive voice.

My voice has been reactive for many years. I may have originally developed it in response to my father's dictum, "You either have it or you don't"—a dichotomy that gave me little choice but to prove him wrong. Or I may have developed it in reaction to my mother's attempt to tame my spirit and bring me in line. The voice I have cultivated as a writer has been an academic voice, a teacher's voice. That is quite different from a memoirist's voice, which demands bare-bones honesty, vulnerability, faithfulness. An academic's voice plays it safe, hiding behind degrees. It says, Think with me about this—not *feel* with me.

But I've noticed my own voice is changing, changing because I want to find the voice that disappeared so many years ago with the need to protect myself from my mother's anger. I want to find the storyteller. I know it will take time, but that voice has been waiting there for me to listen to her stories. I gently coax her out of hiding, pledging to guarantee her safety. We are tentative with each other; she has no reason to trust me yet.

This morning, while out walking first thing after the birds

wake me up, as has become my custom, I start to mourn for my mother. Maybe it is a result of writing about the stories she never felt entitled to tell, or about her bracelet, her hats or massaging her back. Whatever the reason, as I walk along the sea with the oil platforms in the distance and the dolphins occasionally skimming the cresting waves, I start to weep.

I weep for the English garden she proudly planted, which she said my father ripped out, citing the delicacy and short life span of columbines and delphiniums and his preference for hardier rhododendrons. I weep for the Shakespeare volume she secretly and excitedly bought for his seventy-fifth birthday, which he returned the very next day. I weep for her tears over his sale of the oceanfront Florida condo she loved, so that he could build them a house with too many rooms.

I weep for the fact that she died from Alzheimer's without ever knowing what had robbed her of her memories because my father and the doctor wanted to spare her more distress. I am ashamed to admit that my sister and I went along with them. I weep for all the years I listened to stories of my father's heroics and never asked my mother about hers. I weep for the image I cultivated of her as the enemy—a woman who became madder, sadder and more defeated, lacking the agency to live her own life. I weep for the loss of her voice.

Women Writing Their Lives

The other begins not at the skin, as I had thought, but within.

—Inga Clendinnen, *Tiger's Eye*

My mother and I shared the same birthday, two days after Christmas, a mixed blessing for the entire family. I always felt like I had unwittingly horned in on her special day, especially after she informed me that her favorite dog, Lady, died of a broken heart after she brought me home from the hospital. It was not an auspicious beginning to our relationship. I never enjoyed my birthday as a child, because I spent it celebrating my mother's, and she was always disappointed with her gifts, especially last-minute purchases like the white eyelet peignoir from my father. When I pointed out that the design of the white eyelet was beautiful, she blurted out, "He bought that to please himself!"

As my parents approached their late seventies, I tried to persuade them to draw up their wills; I suspected that they weren't going to live forever, no matter how strong-minded they both were. Six years ago, on my mother's and my birthday, my father called me into his study. He and my mother were sitting on the sofa with papers spread out on the glass table in front of them. They both looked serious. The last time I had been summoned to sit down and talk with them was forty years before, when they told me they were going to have another baby. That time I sat on my father's lap; this time I didn't think that was appropriate.

They wanted to talk about their wills. My heart leapt to my throat. This was the conversation I never thought we'd have, and now that we were having it, I was scared. My denial about their mortality turned out to be as strong as theirs.

They explained that they had set up a generation-skipping trust for my children and those of my sister, and they detailed how their monies would be divided after their deaths. I looked over the boilerplate document as my father explained that the exact figures would be added later. Our conversation lasted for a short while and then he left the room to answer the phone. My mother looked at me.

"You don't have a very good track record with men," she started. I wondered where this conversation was leading—my love life had always been a sore subject. Yes, I had just ended the second of my eleven-year marriages, but that didn't necessarily mean I didn't have a good track record. It just meant that those particular races had reached the limit of their endurance.

"You're too trusting," she continued. "You give too much of yourself away. You don't protect yourself well enough."

It was true that both of my ex-husbands got away without paying me alimony, but my first divorce occurred in the late 1970s, when no card-carrying feminist would even *think* of asking for alimony. My mother was right: I didn't protect myself well. Years later, my first husband's law partner told me that my ex had been able to devote himself to pro bono legal work for poor people because I was such a good provider for our children. My second husband's income was not much higher than mine, so my request for alimony was denied.

"Now, it's okay with me if you have a companion, a friend to go to the movies or dinner with. But your father and I don't want you to marry again. Quite frankly, I don't want any man getting hold of my money!"

I had to bite the insides of my mouth not to burst out laughing. You would have thought she was one of the Rockefellers and had accrued an enormous estate! She must have thought I would be surrounded by gold diggers the moment she died. I hadn't lived with her for over thirty years, and here she was telling me what to do with my body.

This was the same woman who imposed a midnight curfew until I was married at twenty-one, so I should have expected some directives. She would wait up until I got home and flick the front porch lights on and off, on and off, immediately after my soon-to-be husband and I pulled into the driveway. The lights flashed frantically if we dallied long enough for a goodnight kiss, and never stilled until I got out of the car and slunk into the house. Her vigilance did not, however, prevent me from getting pregnant.

I told her I didn't have any prospects for marriage, and we put the will away and drove to the beach to go for a walk. My mother loved to look for shells. She used to scour the South Jersey shore for variegated shells to decorate wicker Kleenex boxes and matching wastebaskets. She collected coral from Florida and sprayed it the color of her bathroom wallpaper. She decorated eight successive houses as my father's advertising agency sold more and more prescription drugs. "Your father's never satisfied," she'd moan as she looked through wallpaper books and picked out paints for trim. She was bold with color, painting her last dining room raspberry red.

Seven years ago my father decided to sell their condo on the beach and bought a lot on the Inland Waterway, where he wanted to build a mansion. They had come to visit me in California for Thanksgiving, and when he showed me the architect's plans for their new house, my mother broke down and cried. She had never said no to him before; she had always just complained. This time she couldn't stop the tears.

"Dad, Mom doesn't want to move," I said, giving voice to what seemed obvious.

"She'll love it," he said.

"No, she loves the condo. Don't make her move again. I haven't even seen the condo yet, but I know she loves walking on the beach."

"She'll love decorating the house," he said. "It's actually her idea."

I looked at my mother crying, leaning on the arm of my living-room couch. It was clear that she didn't want to move, and it was also clear that she couldn't fight him anymore. Her entire life had been about giving in to my father, and she had always been furious about it. Now, she was numb.

They lived in the Big House for three years. She hated every minute of it. Two short Irish people living in a sixty-five-hundred-square-foot house; they never stopped shouting for each other from one end of the Georgian-style mausoleum to the other. Every time

I phoned, she'd yell "*Matt!*" in my ear as loud as she could. "He must be at the other end of the house," she'd say. "He'll have to call you back."

That birthday, after the "track record" conversation, I watched my mother shuffle down the beach. She stretched out her arms like a swooping seagull as my own daughter had done when she was four. "I used to do this when I took an exercise class," my mother said, smiling. I knew that she'd never stepped foot in any class where someone would be in a position to tell her what to do with her body. But I just smiled.

In the next moment, she abruptly turned to face the sea and ran into the water with no thought for her safety. I ran after her, grabbed her by the waist and pulled her out of the water before the waves knocked her down. She giggled. I was frightened by her seeming lack of awareness that she had just endangered herself. Her reaction was that of a delighted child. It was then I began to realize that my mother and I were entering new terrain.

A memoir is a slice of life about which a writer muses, struggling to achieve some understanding of a particular life experience. A successful memoir demonstrates a writer's slow coming to awareness, some reckoning with herself over time, some understanding of how her unconscious is at work. Because of this reckoning, the writing of memoir is not without pain. A memoir that successfully taps the reservoir of universal human feeling resonates strongly with its readers.

Lyden's memoir about her mother's manic-depressive illness is a powerful example of emotional complexity, and echoes my own experience. Although my mother was never diagnosed manic-depressive like Lyden's, there were similarities in our mothers' inexplicable behavior. As a child, I longed to understand what provoked my mother's mood changes; I never knew who I would find when I got home from school. My mother could be a gorgeous, charming woman, decked out in furs, pearls and fine clothes, putting on her "face" as she got ready to drive into Manhattan to meet my father for dinner with clients. Or she could be a harridan pushing a vacuum cleaner around the house in a flurry, complaining about how many toilet bowls she had to clean and lashing out at me—who did I think I was, coming home from school fifteen minutes late?

"Take off your shoes, don't track mud into the house, don't give me that look. If you're going to cry, I'll give you something to cry about. Go to your room and stay there."

Other days when I got home, she would be ironing my father's shirts in front of the television, laughing out loud at the antics of Lucy and Ethel on *I Love Lucy,* and I would be invited to sit with her and share her delight in the tricks Lucy and Ethel played on Ricky and Fred. I never knew, when I opened the back door, whether I was going to be viewed as the enemy or an ally.

I created a ritual to deal with the threshold guardian at the gate. Each day on the way home from school, I stopped at the candy store to buy her a Heath bar. That combination of chocolate and toffee seemed to soothe her, and perhaps it gave me a sense of protection. I could tell what kind of afternoon it was going to be when I opened the back door. If the scent of cigarette smoke greeted me at the door, she was probably having a Miller

High Life, her four o'clock beer. In that case, she would be relaxed for a while and I would be safe. I'd save the candy bar for the next day. If I didn't smell the cigarette smoke at the threshold, I'd call out, "Mom, I'm home. I have a surprise for you!"

That's why Lyden's narrative struck such a strong chord in me. She writes that one Christmas night, when she was an adult, her grandmother phoned to tell her that her mother had disappeared. Her disappearance wasn't completely out of the ordinary; her mother often eluded them for days when she was in one of her manic phases. But her grandmother was worried, so Lyden drove to her mother's house to check on her.

> Her home was as dark as Calvary. I crept into the house del-icately, listening, letting the door swing open and calling out to her. She could be dangerous in the dark. "Mom," I shouted at the door. "Are you here? Answer me if you are!" I stayed there, trembling. When I was little I used to sing to my mother, "I love you a bushel and a peck, a hug around the neck." I hummed it now in my head, past the dark, past the blue demons I was sure lined the hall. I sang loudly, making the notes dance toward the basement and up the stairs. A hundred bushels and a thousand pecks, I do, I do.

As a little girl, I too sang that song on the way home from the candy store. Walking down the tree-canopied street, I thought that if I could make my mother happy, she wouldn't get angry. I didn't realize at the time that I was trying to mollify the frustrated beast inside her. In fact, it wasn't until two years ago, when my sister and I happened to be discussing our mutual preference for Ben & Jerry's Coffee Heath Bar Crunch ice cream that we discovered that she too had always brought our mother Heath bars after school. It was then that I understood the full meaning of the ritual. It gave me chills.

"Had you seen me doing the same thing when you were a little girl?" I asked my sister.

"Nope, I just thought it would make her happy and then she wouldn't yell at me."

Three little girls, trying to make their mommies love them. A bushel and a peck, I do, I do.

Lyden's poetic exploration of the world she enters to discover her mother's mental landscape gave me a context for my own decades-long search to understand my mother. When Lyden writes, "The damage grows inside, where you can only sense what is unseen, spreading like moss, or a spiked vine creeping over the brain and flaring down to the tongue," I know exactly what she means. The fear and loathing I sometimes felt for my mother as a child turned into compassion and love as I witnessed the invisible kudzu strangle her mind.

We all have conflicted feelings about our parents. Even young children in the throes of hero worship experience both fierce attachment and crushing disappointment. Diski's memoir is a powerful example of this as she reminisces about her earliest memory of father love. On her third birthday, Diski's parents took her to see Danny Kaye at the Palladium. They sat in the front row and Danny Kaye picked her out of the audience to come up on stage, where he sang a song to her. During the intermission, she was taken back to his dressing room, where she sat on his lap and drank her first Coke. He enchanted her with his kind, funny personality, and at that moment, she felt loved by him.

One day several weeks later, Diski and her father were walking down the street and suddenly, she recalls, she became overcome with longing for Danny Kaye. More than anything else in the world, she wanted *him* to be her father. As she walked along, holding the hand of her actual father, whom she adored, she was overwhelmed by the need to have this other father whom she had known for only a few minutes. She began to cry, knowing that Danny Kaye could never, in fact, be her father.

She was in an impossible situation: She couldn't stop crying, and she couldn't tell her father why she was crying because, she felt, to do so would hurt his feelings. She continued to cry the whole way home and cried herself to sleep that night without ever telling anyone what was wrong.

Shortly thereafter she had another experience of longing for a different father. She woke up one night to hear a violent shouting match between her parents. She went to their room and stood in the doorway. When they saw her, they stopped and asked her what was wrong. She asked them why they were shouting. Her father told her they weren't shouting and said that sometimes adults had conversations that were very loud. He assured her nothing was wrong and told her to go to bed. She knew he was lying.

I suppose it was the first lie I knew about. I remember the shock, and not arguing but going back to bed, pretending

that I believed him. I loved my father more than I could say,
but I don't think I really believed what he told me after that.

In writing about these memories, Diski plumbs the paradoxical
nature of her remembered feelings as a child: her deep longing, at
three years old, for something that she would never have from her
father—the sustained unconditional love and attention of a larger-
than-life archetypal "father"—as well as guilt over wanting a
father other than her own. That longing for something she could
never have is universal; we have all experienced some variation on
the theme of unrequited desire. The fact that Diski grappled with
the complexity of her toddler feelings makes her an effective memoirist. She was willing to glean as much understanding from a particular event as she could.

Each memoirist has a different purpose in undertaking the
writing of memoir, but each attempts the risky task of excavating
specific events in order to understand the truth of her life. Diski
seeks to understand her longing for "father" in recalling an early
memory about Danny Kaye; Lyden seeks to understand her love for
her mother in the midst of her chaotic Christmas landscape. I seek
to disentangle my voice from the grip of my mother's anger.

Lauren Slater challenges the reader to examine the nature of truth
as she constructs her memory in *Lying*. She writes what she calls her
"metaphorical memoir" in such a way that the reader never knows
whether her account of her struggle with epilepsy is reliable or
whether she uses epilepsy as a literary device to explore her state of
being. She begins her memoir by informing the reader that she

exaggerates. "I exaggerate. I have epilepsy. Or I feel I have epilepsy. Or I wish I had epilepsy, so I could find a way of explaining the dirty, spastic glittering place I had in my mother's heart."

Slater recounts her experience of epilepsy and its treatment from her initial seizure when she was ten years old until she is a young adult. She takes us on a journey to neurologists, psychiatrists, a school for epileptics in Kansas where nuns teach her how to fall during a seizure, through the betrayal of adolescent friendships, the loss of her virginity with her mentor at Bread Loaf Writers' Conference, and the loneliness of a confused young woman seeking community in an Alcoholics Anonymous meeting she finds in a church.

She asks the reader to confront the veracity of the masks we each wear; the stories we tell about ourselves, our families, our lovers; what we do for attention, affection and acceptance; and how we make our way in the world. She challenges us to examine how we come to identify ourselves, whether, in her case, as a lonely, confused adolescent, a liar, an epileptic, an alcoholic or a memoirist.

> Why is what we feel less true than what is? Supposing I simply feel like an epileptic, a spastic person, one with a shivering brain; supposing I have chosen epilepsy because it is the most accurate conduit to convey my psyche to you? Would this not still be a memoir, *my memoir*?

Slater poses important questions about identity and truthfulness. She believes that the purpose of a memoir is to capture the *essence* of the narrator rather than the factual details of the life she recounts.

She believes, like Kierkegaard, that the "greatest lie of all is the feeling of firmness beneath our feet." She uses the metaphor of epilepsy and the process of learning how to fall during a seizure to illustrate her need to surrender to the fact that there is really nothing solid in life we can count on. Not even, or perhaps, not in particular, our own self-proclaimed "truth." We are pattern-making creatures, creating stories and metaphors to fill the existential emptiness we all share.

Even though Slater never reveals to the reader whether she is in fact an epileptic, she sanctions her self-identification as such when she writes:

> We create all sorts of lies, all sorts of stories and metaphors, to avoid the final truth, which is the fact of falling. Our stories are seizures. They clutch us up, they are spastic grasps, they are losses of consciousness. Epileptics, every one of us; I am not alone.

Heath Bars, a Girdle and Danny Kaye

Through metaphor, the past has the capacity to imagine us, and we it.

—Cynthia Ozick, *Metaphor and Memory*

The deepest memoir is filled with metaphor. A metaphor uses one thing to suggest another: a Heath bar becomes an offering to appease the mother; Danny Kaye becomes the universally desired idealized father; epilepsy becomes a reminder that there is no safety net in life; a girdle becomes an expression of female bondage. We may not understand what something means in certain circumstances until a metaphor makes it clear. A metaphor transforms the strange, the unknown, into the familiar.

Food writer and memoirist Ruth Reichl discovered that food was the metaphor that helped her make sense of her world. She grew up in New York with a mother who was both unable to taste and unafraid of rot. Reichl spent her young life protecting her mother's guests and her own friends from eating her mother's unsavory and dangerous concoctions. Her mother was insensitive to the fact that many people could not tolerate the mold and spoilage she herself could stomach. After a family dinner she prepared to welcome her son's fiancée into the family, Reichl's mother was dismissive when informed that twenty-six of her guests had to have their stomachs pumped.

> "Really?" she said, sounding shocked. "All of them?" She slumped a little as her bright red fingernails went from her hair to her mouth. Then her back straightened and her head shot up. "Nonsense," I heard her say into the phone. "We all feel fine. And we ate *everything*."

In her hilarious memoir, *Tender at the Bone*, Reichl finds that food can be dangerous, especially to those who love it, and she takes this very seriously. Because her parents entertain a great deal, Reichl appoints herself guardian of the guests by the time she is ten to prevent any premature deaths from her mother's cooking. In a larger sense, guardian of the guests becomes her lifelong vocation.

As a young food sleuth, Reichl learns to pay attention to people's taste in food and their dining preferences. By listening to their conversations about food she discovers clues to their personalities. All of these skills she develops as a child serve Reichl well when she becomes the food critic first for the *Los Angeles Times* and then later for the *New York Times*.

Of course, Reichl's mother's inability to provide healthy food for her family becomes a metaphor for her inadequacy in providing maternal sustenance, but Reichl is fortunate to have two other women in her young life who impart recipes for life along with their preparation of food. Her Aunt Birdie's cook, Alice, who makes the best apple dumplings with hard sauce in the world, teaches six-year-old Ruth the three secrets to a good fried oyster and introduces her to the comforts of the rituals of the kitchen.

Mrs. Peavey, "the world's most improbable maid," comes to live with Ruth and her parents when she is eight. Mrs. Peavey has white-blue hair and a patrician manner, and speaks three languages fluently. In addition to teaching Ruth how to make her father's favorite dish, Wiener schnitzel, by pounding the veal thin and heating the oil hot, Mrs. Peavey gives Ruth three important pieces of advice before she finally quits: Don't let other people tell you how to live your life. You have to look out for yourself. And don't forget the extra pastry when you make beef Wellington. With that, Mrs. Peavey reaches out and hugs Ruth good-bye. The practical, loving advice of these two unique women launch Reichl's career as a food connoisseur.

The metaphors we choose in the writing of memoir take us to a deeper level of knowing the self. The self is not an entity already formed, but an awareness in process. The metaphor we use to tease that awareness into consciousness is what makes the narrative interesting.

A small life like my mother's becomes a metaphor for what is happening to women everywhere. When I look at my mother's desperate attempt to control her body and, by extension, mine, I see the root issue for so much of the feminine experience: the silencing and control of a woman's body. My mother's metaphor was her girdle.

A girdle is tight, it constricts, it creates an illusion of slimness; it prevents the flopping of buttocks or belly, the jiggling of thighs. A girdle restricts breathing, cuts off circulation; it tames sensuality, squelches spontaneity, numbs feelings. No heart beats below the waist when one is girdled. "Beware," it shouts, "I am impenetrable."

My mother's girdle became a metaphor for her rules, her rigidity, her adherence to the Catholic Church. Flashing lights at the threshold to prevent necking, no kissing before marriage. What was she afraid of? What could have terrified her so that she refused to live her life and tried to prevent me from living mine? After all, we wear armor out of fear. When my mother danced the Charleston in her later years, it wasn't with joy and abandon. She danced it with a vengeance. She grabbed my hand so tight it hurt.

I don't believe that she was always so armored. I don't want to believe it. I look at old sepia-toned photos I found in her trunk, and there she is, a young woman riding a horse in the country or sitting on a blanket at some unknown lake with friends. I see a woman at ease with herself, enjoying life. Her face is open, her smile wide. She is still breathing; she has not yet become corseted. The memory of bondage has not settled in. I think that as she aged, life disappointed her so that she girded herself against that revelation.

Women's bodies have long been a metaphor for desire, control and shame. In some cultures, even now, a woman who is sexually active or becomes pregnant outside of marriage is stoned to death or her identity is obliterated through deliberate forgetfulness. In *The Woman Warrior,* Maxine Hong Kingston writes about No Name Woman, an aunt her family tries to expunge by deliberately forgetting her.

This aunt brings disgrace to the family and their Chinese village by having an illegitimate child. She then drowns the child and herself.

No Name Woman performs this act of self-annihilation in direct response to the destruction the villagers inflict on her family's home as punishment for her sexual transgression. Thus, not only does her sexuality not belong to her, but it is the property of her family, which is shamed and punished for her expression of it.

Kingston does not actually have a memory of this aunt, but she constructs one in her memoir. She attempts to recreate her through a combination of her imagination and a memory told to her by her mother. Her aunt's presence in Kingston's life is just as palpable or perhaps even more so than if she had experienced her alive. No Name Woman becomes a cautionary tale for all women about the desire to control the female body.

Laying Down the Veil

In thinking about a metaphor for my own life, I began to realize that my metaphor is closely entangled with my mother's. That doesn't surprise me, but it saddens me that it has outlived her. As Vivian Gornick writes in *The Situation and the Story,* "I could not leave my mother because I had become my mother."

My metaphor is not a girdle but another type of restraint: a habit. A black-and-white habit. My mother always wanted me to become a nun, to "take the veil" as was the euphemism in the late fifties. In fact, I can't remember a time when she didn't glow with pride when telling her friends that I had been "called." The idea of my becoming a nun gave her so much pleasure that I wanted to do it for her. I would become a nun if it would make her happy.

Our house was always filled with propaganda. Pamphlets from missionary orders like the Maryknoll Sisters and books on the lives of the saints: Saint Teresa, the Little Flower, a young beauty looking beatific holding roses in her hands; Saint Elizabeth of Hungary, the queen who left her castle every day to bring bread to the homeless; Father Damien, who risked his life and limbs to care for the lepers; and Saint Francis of Assisi who begged for alms and talked to the birds and animals. These selfless romantic figures hypnotized me as a young girl bent on heroics.

My mother was not by nature a happy woman, but she brightened in the company of nuns and priests. And because my uncle was a priest, they were around our house a lot. She admired them for having a vocation; after all, they were called to do something important in life. They mattered. The implicit message was that being a wife and mother didn't matter and if I didn't do something important, I would never matter either.

So I became driven to be a "good girl," to make a difference, to be outstanding. Although I did not enter the convent, I metaphorically took the veil. I excelled in school, tutored kids after school, tallied the church collection on Sundays. I had my own mission: to save my mother—from her mood swings, from alcohol, from herself. Failing that, I would save the world: the inner-city youth whom I tutored, the Indians with whom I lived and worked as a student missionary in Mexico, the therapy clients I saw in my practice. The metaphoric nun became my driving force.

I don't deny that there are a lot of rewards in taking the invisible veil. It gave me a modicum of authority, respect and accomplishment. But the inner voice of the missionary does not speak for all of me. The combination of zeal and self-righteousness that comes with the black-and-white habit, with black-and-white thinking, constrict me just as much as the girdle constrained her.

The Tiger's Landscape

Inga Clendinnen, Australia's award-winning historian of Aztec and Mayan civilizations, was immobilized by an incurable liver disease in her early fifties. As she lay for months in a hospital bed, she turned to her memories and imagination as a refuge from the debilitation of her body. Out of that experience came *Tiger's Eye,* an extraordinary memoir about the working of memory and the construction of self.

Clendinnen chronicles what it is to lie still in a hospital bed feeling the disintegration of her mind, fearing the disintegration of her self and trying to understand the transformation of her body as it wastes away. She explores not only what it is to lose her known identity, but also what it is to discover an expanded identity that begins to unfold in her imagination. One night as she lies in her hospital bed terrified by the prospect of dying, she hears a familiar sound outside the walls of her enclosure, the sound of zoo lions roaring. She had forgotten that the zoo is close to the hospital, separated by a mere stretch of parkland. There, in her imagination, she quickly joins the animals, visiting one species after another. Listening to the lions, she begins to hear a sound that she had not needed to remember until then: "a dark crimson vibration, a sensation in the diaphragm: the low, rumbling, sighing cough of the tiger."

Clendinnen reveals that her favorite beast is the tiger, because he is the only animal who does not acknowledge living in a cage. She imagines his royal sweep:

> He would pace its length, the huge body moving smooth as an oiled machine, head carried low and level, searchlight eyes absolutely steady, and then at the corner would come the lunging pivot, the blinding turn within the single body length, and he would be padding back the other way, his indifferent gaze sweeping bars, lawns, people, keepers, and dismissing them utterly. Incidents in a tiger landscape.

This imaginary visit to the tiger landscape gives Clendinnen hope. Lying in a hospital bed, she too feels caged, with keepers, feeding times, bars at the side of her bed and the horror of helplessness on the horizon. But the vision of the tiger inspires her. Like him, she does not have to capitulate to a state of helplessness. Instead, she can look out of her confinement through the tiger's eye and invoke the vision of freedom it gives her. Whenever she feels the threat of losing her self to her illness, she enters the tiger landscape to "be at once the superb gaze, and the object of the gaze: an incident in a tiger landscape." Through his beauty and wholeness, the tiger frees her from the terror of wasting away.

Clendinnen's use of imagination and fantasy frees the prospective memoirist from the spell of historical and literal "truth." What matters in knowing and writing herself is Clendinnen's narrative truth. As her illness progresses, she invites the reader into her inner landscape occasioned by involuntary hallucinations brought on by certain medications used in her treatment. She names these visions the "unauthorized version" of her mind and memory.

> I did not "invent" the hallucinations. These communiqués from my dark interior had long existed, like ancient flints, deep inside me. Now they had worked their way to the light. Only by playing historian to my nightmares would I be able to negate their power.

Clendinnen realizes that she will never look upon herself in the same way after these terrifying visions. Having a successful liver transplant and returning home to family and friends, she knows they assume she has come back to them as before. She can see it in their eyes. They expect her to be her old self. But she is different; she now knows what she is made of:

> Just a ragbag of metaphors, a hank of memories and a habit of interrogation, held together by drugs. And if you say "Aha! What then is this observing and commenting 'I'?" I answer that it is a shred, a nothing: a sliver of shattered silk whirling in the wind, without anchor or destiny, surviving only because the wind happened to drop.

Clendinnen's poetic metaphor is not self-deprecating; it is a humbling thought for anyone, much less a scholar who relies so tenaciously on her factual mind, to experience herself as a sliver of shattered silk whirling in the wind. Most of us spend much of our lives layering the garments of our different roles to build up the fictions of our imagined destinies. We don't want to know the extent of our fragility in the face of death. To peel the fictions of our created lives is an act of supreme courage, viewed by some as lunacy. We might have to agree with Slater that the greatest lie of all is the illusion of firmness beneath our feet.

By recounting her dance with death and the unknown chambers of her mind, Clendinnen challenges the reader to think about what is real in life and what is the fiction we create.

> I was beginning to suspect, after my drug-induced thrashings and wallowings, that we are fictions too: not coherent and continuous objects in a changing sea, but half-illusory creatures made out of the light and shadows cast by that sea, articulated by our own flickering imaginations.

Clendinnen suspects that memory is made up of more than the conscious experiences of our personal past. It contains as well the vast chamber of our personal unconscious: the dreams, images and metaphors that enlarge our lives. Perhaps, too, the memories, dreams and reflections of the whole collective, tigers and human alike. In doing so, she gives the writer a larger lens to view the landscape. A tiger's eye.

Don't Bother

We are all trying to find a past that belongs to us. To assure ourselves that we are not alone. Thinking we can shed light on the darkness that was the world before our birth, that will be the world after our death.

—Mary Gordon, *The Shadow Man*

*I*n the weeks before her death, my mother found a lightness of being and a sense of humor that had previously escaped her. She assured me that golf was everything, even though she had rarely played, informed my sister she was thirsty and wanted champagne, even though she could barely swallow water, and said, "Let's have a party. I want a band."

Rosemary and I both flew to my parents' home in Florida three weeks before my mother died, when the hospice nurse called to say that Mom had taken a turn for the worse. She was experiencing terminal anxiety. She alternated between the terror of not knowing what was happening to her brain, saying, "I think I'm going crazy," to the certainty that, although bedridden, she would dance again. She gave us glimpses of what she saw beyond.

"I have a new room with Joe," she said about her brother, who had died two years earlier. She talked directly to saints we could not see and commiserated with the Virgin Mary. "It must have been so hard for you growing up Jewish," this Irish Catholic woman said.

She slept fitfully that weekend. She was gripped with anxiety, her eyes wide open with fright. She saw a little boy standing at the foot of her bed and took no comfort when my sister escorted the specter out of her bedroom. She assured Rosemary that he would not leave.

When she was awake and lucid, we took turns having our children speak to her on the phone. Sometimes she would nod her head; mostly she just smiled as she listened to their voices. Or she would slowly say, "Love you too." Dad could not accept that she was in the final stages of her disease and refused to talk about funeral arrangements, but Rosemary and I persisted by making reading selections she would have liked for her funeral Mass.

Dad cared for Mom at home during her rapidly progressing battle with Alzheimer's. He was sure, in his words, that she could "beat it." Although he hired caretakers for her during the day, his sleep was compromised by her night terrors. "Matt," she would call out at all hours of the night. And he would respond, "I'm here, sweetheart. I'm here."

He developed a chronic cold. My sister listened with her stethoscope to the congestion gathering in his chest; she feared that he had developed pneumonia. We decided that I would extend my stay through the weekend to take him to his doctor on Monday. A stubborn man, he refused to go.

When he heard me on the phone with the doctor's nurse, he picked up the other phone. "I'll be fine," he said gruffly to the nurse when she suggested he come right in. He slammed down the phone and told me to mind my own business. I went into my mother's room, completely frustrated. She was asleep.

"Mom, I need your help," I said aloud as I sat by her bedside. I couldn't remember ever having asked my mother for help before; it wasn't part of our relationship. The words felt foreign on my tongue, but I asked because I didn't know what else to do.

"Mom, Dad is really acting like a bad boy," I continued. "Rosemary and I think he's got pneumonia and I can't get him to go see the doctor. He just won't cooperate. Tell me what to do."

I didn't really think she could hear me. She hadn't responded or uttered a sound in the previous twelve hours. She was barely breathing. I sat there for a while, as was my custom, holding her small hand.

Her fingers moved under my touch; her eyelids fluttered and slowly opened. It took some time for her eyes to focus. She looked as if it had been a great struggle to bring her attention back to the living. It was as if she had been away for a long while.

"Don't bother," she said slowly, as she scanned my face. I laughed and then stared at her, startled by what she had said. "Don't bother?" I repeated to myself as her eyelids closed. "Don't bother?" I ask you for advice and you tell me, "Don't bother"? I waited for her to say more. But there was no more to be said.

She had been married to this man for fifty-five years. She had tried her best to weather the whims of his creative will. One time she had said to me, "If I had known your father was so ambitious, I never would have married him." Who knew better the nature of the beast? What my mother said about trying to change my father was the best advice she could give.

The hospice nurse called me on the phone two weeks later to tell me that Mom's color and vital signs were good, but she doubted that my mother would live through the end of the week. My sister had called me the night before.

"She'll probably go on Thursday, on the feast of the Ascension," said Rosemary. "Special souls take off on feast days, you know. Are you going to go?"

"I don't think so. I already said my good-byes. Do you want me to go?"

"I would feel better if you would, but I don't want to ask you to go."

My sister and I had talked before about being present for our mother's death. She knew that she didn't want to see our mother die. We both knew that our father couldn't accept that Mom would ever go. I thanked Rosemary for her clarity and hung up.

I didn't want to go back, because I didn't want to make the eight-hour trip across the continent that I had just made two weeks before. I didn't want to go, because my latest book had just been published and I had a bookstore reading scheduled the next night. I didn't want to go, because my mother and I had made our peace with each other, and part of me felt that she would go on forever. Her mother had just died four years earlier at one hundred years old. I didn't want to go, because I was afraid that it would be another false alarm. We had already had four. I didn't want to go, because I was afraid to see my mother die.

I arrived on the Feast of the Ascension at 5 P.M. Mom was alone in her bedroom, oxygen easing her breathing. The hospice nurse met me at the front door and said my father was out getting food.

She told me to prepare myself for the changes that had occurred in Mom in the seventeen days since I had last seen her. At that time her skin had been beautiful, rosy and smooth. My sister had marveled at the absence of wrinkles in her complexion. She seemed to be getting younger as each brain cell died.

I wasn't prepared for the color in her face and hands. The nurse hadn't told me her fingernails had turned blue. Her face was gray and each breath was labored. Her eyes were neither open nor closed. Just glassy.

"Mom, it's Maureen," I said. "I'm here." She grunted a long sigh of recognition. Or maybe she was just struggling to breathe. I chose to take it as a sign of recognition as my own breath caught in my throat with the sound of her gasps. I held her hand in mine and smoothed her hair and sweaty brow. "Mom, I hate to see you suffer so. It breaks my heart. I'm so sorry we had such a tumultuous relationship."

There, I said it. This was the one thing I had never said. I had waited for years to hear her say, "I'm sorry," but I hadn't realized that the reason I had flown three thousand miles was to apologize to her. It had never entered my mind. Another long sigh, this time, perhaps of relief. It's strange how we grasp, even at the end, for our mother's validation.

I had been reading *The Tibetan Book of the Dead* on the plane, and it described how hearing is the last sense to go. I put my hand on my mother's heart and spoke gently into her ear. "It's okay, Mom, you can let go now. Everyone is going to be okay. Dad's okay, Rosemary's okay. Juli and Cristin and Heather and Brendan are okay too. Kiki is okay. She's asleep right here on the chair, purring.

You don't have to struggle anymore. You can let go. Just let yourself move toward the light."

She continued to sweat and wheeze. Her eyes never moved. I continued to speak in her ear. Then I sat back and took her hand, which was so soft and small. I looked at her fingers, her nails transparent yet blue. I don't know where the impulse came from, but I started to sing "My Wild Irish Rose," making up lyrics where I had forgotten the words. Her breathing started to soften, to slow down, to relax. I alternated telling her to move toward the light and singing for the next half hour, stopping only when my father came back with pizza.

"Dad, what are the words to 'My Wild Irish Rose'? I can't remember them."

He started to sing too. We sang together off-key for a couple of rounds, and I said irreverently, "This will surely kill her if nothing else does." He smiled and said, "Come and eat some pizza while it's still hot."

I told him I'd be there in a bit. I wasn't ready to leave. One of my writing students had just read a piece in class the night before about being in the kitchen making a sandwich when his father died alone in the living room. It didn't seem right to eat; I didn't want her to slip away while we were in the kitchen eating pizza. Dad kissed Mom's forehead and left the room.

Something changed. The air. Her breathing. The light. I don't know exactly what it was, but it was palpable. I kept telling her to move toward the white light, but then the color seemed to change to blue. "Move toward the blue light, Mom. Mother Mary has her arms stretched out to you. She's waiting for you. Take her hand."

Her breathing relaxed. Time stopped. We stayed that way for I don't know how long, maybe seconds, maybe minutes, certainly no more. Then my stomach started to growl. "Mom, I'm going to get a piece of pizza. I'll have one for you." She grunted. Or maybe I just thought she did so I could leave. She actually made no sound at all.

The hospice nurse replaced me in Mom's bedroom, and Dad and I ate our pizza reminiscing about big, thick, juicy slices of pizzas of years past. The best were always at Stasney's, a small Italian restaurant in northern New Jersey. After we ate our third piece of pizza, the hospice nurse came out of Mom's bedroom. "I think you might want to go in to her, Mr. Hennessey. Her breathing has changed."

My father went in and the nurse closed their bedroom door. I panicked. I started to pace outside their door in the hallway. I wanted to go in, but the door to their room was closed. "Give him some time," the hospice nurse said to me gently.

I looked for my camera. I just wanted to take their picture one more time. My film jammed as I tried to load it; I couldn't get it to advance.

Dad's camera didn't seem to work either. I picked up a generic Instamatic that was sitting on the mahogany sideboard and opened their bedroom door. I stopped at the threshold. Dad was holding Mom's hand and all was quiet. I took their picture. The flash went off. He turned his head to me. "I think she's gone," he said.

I walked over to her hospital bed and put my hand on the side of her neck. Her pulse was still. I nodded. "You're right, Dad. She's gone." My father looked up at me in dismay. "How could she?" he said, his eyes filled with the look of a man betrayed. He got up and slowly walked around to the other bed, a twin, where he had slept these past months keeping her company. He sat down, cradled his head in his hands and started to sob. I went over to hold him and we both cried.

The next thing I remember after calling my sister is crawling into the hospital bed with my mother, holding her and smoothing her hair. I put my hand on her belly, surprised by the warmth of her middle as her hands and lips got progressively colder. I closed her eyes and continued to tell her to move toward the light.

My mother had never let me hold her before.

My mother's death was one of the most peaceful and profound experiences of my life. I held her for a long time after she died. She had become so small; only months before, I had propped her up over the kitchen sink so a friend could wash her hair. Now she felt even smaller, like a newborn, but her spirit filled the room. She was released—she didn't belong to any of us anymore.

I have wondered from time to time about my memory of the blue light and Mother Mary reaching out to her. Did I actually see it or was it my imagination? Since we can't separate imagination from memory, I will never know. My mother was greatly devoted to Mary, so I'm sure it would have been her fondest desire for Mary, in whatever form, to be there for her transition. What I am sure of is the divine energy that was palpable in the room at the time. Even though a debilitating disease robbed my mother of her memory, in the end, it could not take away the core of her being. In some ways, my mother's loss of her mind restored her to her self.

The Healing Power of Memoir

Pain is not easier for having been suffered before in the same way, but it is more bearable for having been narrated.

—Carolyn Heilbrun, *Hamlet's Mother and Other Women*

*I*n writing about an illness or a critical life event, a memoirist has the opportunity to link her feelings, both negative and positive, with the memory. It is not easy to describe the details of pain or trauma at the time it is occurring; the process of healing has not yet begun. A writer needs time and distance to reflect upon her feelings.

Each time I have written about my mother's final hour, I have had the opportunity to reflect upon our relationship and examine my experience of her. Until her death, I had never admitted to myself the part I played in the difficulties in our relationship. My mother was a convenient hook upon which I had hung all my fear, anger and desire; she was a complicated, inconsolable woman. I had tried to understand her and protect myself from her for years and had waited, like so many children do, for some acknowledgment of her culpability. Instead, I found myself asking for her forgiveness. I didn't know how healing this spontaneous outburst had been for me until I put it into writing. I also did not realize, at the time of her death, that she had offered me a glimpse of her life beyond.

When a writer has the courage to host a painful memory, she has the opportunity to make sense of the suffering and confusion it entails. Suffering clarifies identity and connects us with our deepest selves. The expression of suffering, in any form, is often accompanied by shame. But all feelings need expression, and the insights gained from describing a particular passage in life give us the opportunity to grow as human beings. It is the act of writing rather than the writing itself that provides an opportunity to heal. The compassion, regard and deep respect we grow for ourselves and each other is what creates the shift.

I was incredibly moved by *Paula,* Isabel Allende's memoir about the last year of her daughter's life. In her mid-twenties, Paula became gravely ill with porphyria, a rare genetic metabolic disorder, and fell into a coma from which she never recovered. Allende spent that year at her daughter's bedside in Spain fighting for her daughter's life, and writing the story of her family for when Paula would awaken. In the process of trying to maintain her sanity through continuously more grave prognoses about her daughter's condition, Allende writes about the life of her family in Chile before the military takeover that would kill her uncle, President Salvatore Allende, through the family's exile to Venezuela, Paula's romance and marriage to Ernesto and her move with him to Spain. It is in Spain that Paula becomes ill during the first year of their marriage. Allende writes to preserve memory for her daughter as she is losing all the functions of her mind and body.

Writing with the tenacity of a mother who will do everything in her power to keep her daughter alive, Allende never doubts for an instant that her love will ultimately rob death of her child:

> Death laid its hands on you Monday, Paula. It came and pointed to you, but found itself face to face with your mother and grandmother and, for now, has backed off. It is not defeated, and is still circling round, grumbling, in its swirl of dark rags and clicking bones.

Her writing process begins to parallel the process of Paula's deteriorating condition. Sometimes she feels hopeful and writes long passages about their lives together. Other times she feels such despair about her daughter's lack of response to medical interventions that she can barely write a word.

> You have been sleeping for a month now, I don't know how to reach you; I call and call but your name is lost in the nooks and crannies of this hospital. My soul is choking in sand. . . . I plunge into these pages in an irrational attempt to overcome my terror. I think that perhaps if I give form to this devastation I shall be able to help you, and myself, and that the meticulous exercise of writing can be our salvation.

What else can a parent exercise but her own will when she knows that in spite of consulting the leading professionals in the field, there is nothing more she can do to help the one she loves? If she is a passionate writer like Allende, she clings to the hope that if she can put her fierce will into words, she can keep her child alive.

> I place my hands on your head and your breast and try to transmit health and energy. I visualize you inside a glass pyramid, isolated from harm in a magic space where you can get well. I call you all the pet names I have ever given you and tell you a thousand times, I love you, Paula, I love you.

After many months, Allende decides to take Paula out of the hospital in Spain, where the doctors see her condition as hopeless, and fly her home to San Francisco, where she will be surrounded by family. There, Allende contacts a team of doctors, healers and ritualists, determined that she will be able to reverse Paula's condition with their skills and the fresh air of San Francisco Bay. For the next six months, she watches her daughter become more fragile and silent. As Allende becomes increasingly obsessed with saving her daughter and increasingly filled with despair, Paula finally comes to her in a dream and asks her mother to let her go:

> "Listen, Mama, wake up. I don't want you to think you're dreaming. I've come to ask for your help . . . I want to die and I can't . . . if you took my hand it would be easier to cross to the other side—the infinite loneliness of death frightens me. . . . I have lived my time and I want to say goodbye. Everyone in the family understands that but you; I am eager to be free, you're the only one who hasn't accepted the fact that I will never be as I was before."

Paula reassures her mother that she will love her forever and visit her in dreams every night of her life. It is this dream visitation that persuades Allende that it is indeed time to let her daughter go. She and Paula's husband prepare a private ritual of love and release, and the family waits for weeks for the end to come naturally. Paula becomes more and more translucent. The day of her death, they sponge Paula's body, anoint her skin with cologne, dress her in warm clothing so she won't feel cold, put rabbit fur slippers on her feet, comb her long black hair and place photographs of her nephew and niece, who are lying on her feet to keep her warm, in each of her hands.

As Paula's spirit begins to rise from her body, Allende cradles her daughter against her chest as she had when Paula was a young child. The room fills with the spirits of the ancestors whom Allende had written about throughout the year:

> Granny was there in her percale dress and marmalade-stained apron, with her fresh scent of plums and large blue eyes. Tata, with his Basque beret and rustic cane, was sitting in a chair near the bed. Beside him, I saw a small, slender woman with Gypsy features, who smiled at me when our glances met: Meme, I suppose, but I didn't dare speak to her for fear she would shimmer and vanish like a mirage.

Allende imagines herself rising out of her own body holding the hand of her child clinging to the cloth of her dress. But as she tries to cross the threshold with her daughter, she hears the sound of her grandmother Meme's voice calling her back: "No one can go with her, she has drunk the potion of death." Their voyage together ends in an absolute void as her daughter goes on without her and Allende dissolves into life:

> I am everything that exists, I am in every leaf of the forest, in every drop of the dew, in every particle of ash carried by the stream, I am Paula and I am also Isabel, I am nothing and all other things in this life and other lives, immortal. Godspeed, Paula, woman. Welcome, Paula, spirit.

As my mother passed over, I too felt the union with all aspects of life that Allende describes, of being one with God and humankind, just as I had thirty years earlier when I gave birth to my son. The birth canal and the pathway to death are not dissimilar: Each threshold is filled with unfathomable darkness as well as sacramental light.

Healing can occur for the memoirist as she writes about her relationship with another person as well as her internal process. In reality, one cannot be separated from the other. Healing can also occur for a reader as she perceives a writer grappling with a particular memory and coming to some slow awareness of its significance; a relationship forms between the reader and the author and between the reader and her own life. Reading another person's memoir gives the reader the opportunity to reflect upon *her* life's memories, possibilities and chances for renewal. If we can offer each other the comfort and insights of our experience, perhaps what we offer will heal.

I found Bayley's memoir about his experience with his wife's Alzheimer's tremendously helpful, in fact, *healing* for me in understanding so many little things the doctors never told us about the disease, as well as helping me accept my own conflicted feelings about my mother's neediness and my irritation with her helplessness. Yes, it was difficult to be so intimate with my mother's body, particularly in view of her modesty, but after all, she bathed and changed me as a child. It was the least I could do as she regressed.

The fundamental premise of memoir writing is a belief in the restorative power of telling one's truth; once told, the writer can begin to move on with her life. Allende may never have been able to release her daughter without guilt had she not written the story of Paula's life and examined her own role as mother in the process. I may never have been able to release my mother without regret had I not written the story of her transition, in which she so graciously allowed me to participate.

Allende's remembrance of her daughter's death mirrors my own experience of my mother's passage and what a sacred honor it is to witness the invisibles who come to assist with the transition. One of the temporal elements of death that unnerved me at the time of my mother's death was how quickly cold moves in to replace the embodied spirit. Somehow I thought I would have more time with her warmth. Allende's words echo my own experience: "The cold of death comes from within, like a blazing, internal bonfire; when I kissed her, ice lingered on my lips like a burn."

I had not looked to memoir for healing, but I found it so. It is true that we never know exactly what heals a person, but the greatest healing may come in knowing that from our suffering we have comfort to offer each other and that we are not, in fact, alone.

This is the gift memoir provides: a vehicle for ordinary people like you and me to explore and come to terms with the mysteries and rituals of life and death.

Not to Go Inside

What, then, do I love when I love my God?

—St. Augustine, *Confessions*

Although we have lost our spiritual connection, we have not lost our spiritual desire. In the same way, although we are without gods, they have not disappeared.

—James Hollis, *Archetypal Imagination*

We flew my mother's body to her home parish in New Jersey, where we would have her wake, funeral Mass and burial. My father wanted a top-of-the-line cherry-wood coffin, and my sister picked out one of Mom's brightly colored patterned silk dresses in which to bury her. Rosemary also did Mom's makeup and hair.

We lined the walls of the funeral home with photographs of my mother with family and friends from all stages of her life. I told Dad I wanted to give her friends the opportunity to tell stories about Mom at the wake, as we had at my uncle's rather raucous wake two years earlier. I wanted to hear their reminiscences. My father accused me of trying to orchestrate their grief.

Rosemary and her daughter Cristin prayed the rosary at the open coffin while I greeted the guests as they came into the funeral parlor. I chatted with Mom's friend Sister Anne, whom I had never met before. We discovered that we had attended the same college in Philadelphia in the sixties, but we hadn't crossed paths then because the nuns were segregated from the regular college students. As we talked about our experiences in Philadelphia during that time, Sister Anne told me about the pilgrimage to the Holy Land that she and my mother had enjoyed in the nineties, "walking in the footsteps of Saint Paul." Sister Anne talked lovingly of my mother and of her devotion to Mary.

Her gentle manner touched me, and I found myself telling her that I thought my mother had always been disappointed that I had not entered the convent, that I hadn't followed the call she had so desperately wanted for me and at one time had wanted for herself. After my tree-drawing incident at age five, I had told my mother I wanted to become a nun. Irish Catholic mothers were in the habit, at that time, of offering up one of their children to God, so she had been pleased. Beginning at that tender age, I had walked a mile to early Mass every day before school until I turned fifteen.

As the praying of the rosary grew louder, I told Sister Anne the story of my entrance interview at the Maryknoll novitiate. Caught up with sixties Peace Corps idealism, I had decided to enter Maryknoll with an eye toward serving as a missionary in Africa. In the spring of my senior year in high school I went to the Motherhouse in Ossining, New York, for my interview. My friend Caren drove us in her brand-new green Volkswagen convertible.

We were both curious about the Motherhouse. We howled about the name, wondering what kind of mothers were housed there. When we arrived, the novice mistress and I talked for some time in her office. She explored the basis for my vocation, and I began to understand, perhaps for the first time, the gravity of the path I was choosing.

At the end of our talk she asked me to go into the chapel alone to pray and search my soul to find out if this was truly my calling. There was no doubt in my mind that it was. After all, I had been preparing myself for twelve years. She walked me to the door of the chapel, opened it, and I went inside.

The chapel was quite small, barely lit and empty. It took some moments for my eyes to adjust to the darkness. I slowly started to walk up the center aisle toward the one lonely candle lit on the altar. But as I reached the pew closest to the door from which I had just come, a voice stopped me.

"Turn around. You've already done this before."

I stopped and turned my head to the right, the direction from which the voice had come. There was no one there.

I heard the voice again—above me, below me, inside me. This time it was louder. *"Turn around, you've already done this before."* The voice didn't warn, it didn't plead, it didn't scare me. It just was. This time I obeyed.

I turned around, walked to the door, opened it and bumped right into the nun who had left me there just seconds ago. At chest level. My head grazed the starched white bib she wore over the front of her black habit. I looked up at her and said, "I must go." She didn't question me.

Caren drove us home across the Tappan Zee Bridge, this time with the top down. When I told my mother my decision, she cried for two weeks.

"But you go to Mass every day," she said, "I don't understand."

"I know, Mom. I'm sorry, it's just not right for me."

I had no words for what I had experienced, nothing I could say to relieve her pain. How could I tell my mother that I had heard a *voice* and I knew in my soul that the voice was right? I never told her what had happened; in fact, it was a story I had never told anyone until that night. Sister Anne looked at me and smiled.

"You did follow your call," she said. "Your call was *not* to go inside."

Not to go inside. Her words touched something deep in the core of my being. I burst into tears. It had never occurred to me that a call could work in reverse, that one could be called *not* to do something. I repeated her words several times to myself. My call was not to go inside. I was speechless.

I had always felt guilty about letting my mother down. It was unspoken, but I knew that she felt my decision not to become a nun reflected badly upon her as a mother. Or at least that was the meaning I made out of her tense silence. While her mother had enjoyed special status in the Church because her son became a priest, Mom didn't get to have that. Both my sister and I married and had children. But I never for a moment doubted the voice I heard in the chapel. Thirty-five years later Sister Anne confirmed its truth.

My original decision to become a nun had been entwined with my encounter with the luminosity of the tree I could not draw. My perception of the tree's aliveness was an experience of the numinous, for which I had no words at age five. The institutional Church was not where I belonged. My spirit was too rebellious. I found the sacred in the trees, the creeks and the boulders of my childhood. And, as I later discovered, I was not alone in finding the land alive with soul.

We use various symbols to help us access the sacred aspect of our lives, symbols that provide a context, a container for the mystery beyond everyday life, and also serve to connect us to the images present in our daily life. Considering the importance of our physical milieu to our understanding of the sacred, it is no surprise that the sixteenth-century mystic Teresa of Avila used the inner castle as the metaphor for her spiritual search, since the predominant architectural structures surrounding her in her native Spain were castles.

Early spiritual memoirs, such as Teresa's, and Augustine's *Confessions,* take the form of a dialogue with God, allowing the writer to chart her spiritual progress, examine her conscience and prepare herself for encounters with the divine in prayer and communion. Some contemporary spiritual memoirists instead write about finding the life of spirit in community, in nature, on pilgrimage or in the ordinariness of everyday life. The spiritual quest is no longer the domain solely of the mystics; people of all ages are writing about their longing for "god" and their search for a definition of the sacred value they give life. One of my favorite memoirs in this genre is Anne Lamott's *Traveling Mercies,* in which she discovers God in the ladies' room outside a blood lab in northern California.

Lamott, a single mother of eight-year-old Sam, has just received the news that the findings of her son's blood sample are being sent to an oncologist in San Francisco for review. Sam was treated for parasites they picked up on a trip to Mexico, but the treatment was inconclusive. Lamott has already lost her father and several friends to cancer and is terrified about the thought of losing Sam. To calm herself, she goes into the ladies' room, and it is there that she finds God:

> Maybe God is in the men's room too, but I have been in so few of them since I got sober. At any rate, I sat on the toilet and closed my eyes. It was incredibly quiet. Then Sam began to fill up urine specimen cups with tap water and to do various pouring experiments with them—pouring water from cup to cup when the brims were touching, pouring from one cup to another from many inches away, covering the mouth of one cup with another and trying to transfer the water without spilling any—or, the second time, without spilling so much.

Watching Sam doing his simple Piagetian water experiments, Lamott decides she will deal with her fear by simply showing up and being as sane and faithful and grown-up as she can be. She also decides to pray. As she prays to God for help, the answer she receives is "Go forth and shop."

Lamott obeys. She and Sam go to the toy store next door, where she buys him a plastic toy that transforms from a race car to an armed replicant with legs, tail and head. She goes back to the ladies' room, sits in a stall, closes her eyes and prays what she calls "beggy prayers." She also suggests to God other candidates for illness, for example, "people of dubious political responsibility," but pleads that it not be her boy. As she sits in the stall plagued with ominous thoughts, she gets the image of the prophet Elijah hiding in a dark cave while waiting to be either killed by Ahab or saved by God. While Elijah waited for God, an angel visited him and told him to eat.

Elijah ate hearthcakes and drank water while he waited. Lamott decides to do the same. She takes Sam home, where they rest for two days, drink a lot of water and eat muffins in lieu of hearthcakes. She prays for patience and remembers that when you need to feel God, sometimes the best thing to do is to enjoy the little things in daily life.

So she washes the windows, gives the dog a flea bath, lies on the floor and draws with her son, and watches the sun come through the windows. And waits. When the call finally comes, she finds that her prayers have been answered: First, she has developed patience, and second, Sam does not have cancer. He is finally diagnosed with a nondescript allergy.

Lamott, who has pointedly retained her sense of humor throughout her many personal challenges, is one of the most poignant memoirists of our time. She writes with both pathos and humor, reminding us that when we reach out for a tangible sign of the existence of the sacred, we find our answer in the most unlikely places.

Mary Rose O'Reilley found hers while mucking out the stalls on a sheep farm in Minnesota. O'Reilley lived a full life; she entered the convent at eighteen, only to leave after two years. Later she married, had children, divorced and embraced first Quakerism, then Zen Buddhism. In her spiritual memoir, *The Barn at the End of the World,* she writes about leaving the world of academia as an English professor at midlife and discovering her own spirituality hauling hay, chasing and tacking sheep, herding, haltering, currying, worming, shearing, trimming hoofs, sweeping barn floors and shoveling manure.

> Lots of people fear spirituality because they think it incompatible with natural happiness. They think surrender to God will take something precious away from them. It's no wonder they think this, of course: many religious practices violate our instinctive wisdom. Some skinny guru, covered in ants at the mouth of a cave, does not speak to our survival instincts.

O'Reilley readily admits that her religious nature is "omnivorous." She has a perpetual hunger for guidance and revelation and embraces mentors everywhere who "rise up before me, as though evolved from mist, and show me the way I must go." She finds that she can worship just about anything that occupies a certain slant of light.

She finds God in her everyday life, tending her Hampshires, Dorsets and Polypays, sweeping the barn floor, entering into a meditative state that she, like many others in diverse traditions, believes is essential to spiritual evolution. Her journey leads her to the conclusion that every religious tradition is concerned with the same phenomena: mystery, the desire for understanding, the longing for love and connection, and at the same time, a deep attachment to the earth.

When poet Kathleen Norris returned to the homeland of her Methodist ancestors in western South Dakota after her grandmother died, she did not realize that living on the Great Plains would lead her to a religious frontier where she would be nourished by the fifteen-hundred-year-old tradition of Benedictine monasticism. In *Dakota,* Norris details her move with her poet husband from New York to her family's land to manage the farm interests of her ancestors. In the course of the memoir, her personal search for place becomes a sacred journey.

Norris spends time in various Benedictine retreat houses and is so nourished by the Rule of Saint Benedict that she eventually becomes an oblate, a person who does spiritual work for the monastic order but does not take vows. She also finds that the small voice inside her that initially prompted her to move back to South Dakota is that of her Methodist grandmother, who inhabits her very core. Curious about the faith of her grandmother, she goes back to church, where she not only finds community, but also rediscovers her religious roots.

> I write on the Plains, in a small town. I am indelibly an outsider, because I write and because I spent my formative years away. I am also an insider by virtue of family connection. I have a unique role here and try to respect its complexity. I have no family in the area now, but my roots go deep. When with considerable misgivings I joined my grandmother's Presbyterian church more than ten years after she died, an old woman startled me by saying, "It's good to have a Totten in the church again."

People in the community, such as this old woman, help Norris rediscover her heritage. She believes that the spiritual search of her baby-boomer generation is really a search for place, a search for community: "We are seeking the tribal, anything with strong communal values and traditions. . . . I suspect that when modern Americans ask 'what is sacred?' they are really asking 'what place is mine? What community do I belong to?'" This is the same question addressed by our ancient ones in the mythologies and religions of their time.

However the numinous dimension is defined, each writer finds it in her own way. O'Reilley contemplates the quality of life as she tends her sheep; Norris finds her connection with the sacred through her patient observation of and attunement to the sparse desert plains of her ancestors. For countless pilgrims around the world, it is the divine mother symbolized in so many different forms who for centuries has listened to their prayers and entreaties: the Virgin of Guadalupe, the Black Madonna of Czestochowa, the *Vierge Noire* of Rocamadour, to name just a few.

I never really understood the depth and breadth of this connection to the universal symbol of the mother until I saw a man, a bit worn down by life, stand in front of the Black Madonna in the basilica at Einsiedeln, Switzerland, beseeching her assistance. If you have ever been to Switzerland, you know that you never see a homeless person; this man, however, was disheveled and looked like he had been homeless for some time.

He took off his hat, stretched out his hands and arms in entreaty and loudly cried out his anguish to her before the ushers moved him away. I was startled both by his lack of self-consciousness in pouring his heart out in front of the congregation and by the level of anguish in his prayer. It was clear that he was clinging to a faith that she would hear him and answer his prayers. As a few people joined him in singing the Salve Regina, it was evident that they believed in her as well. It was also sadly apparent to me that I did not share their level of faith.

When I was a young girl, I always knelt in front of the statue of Mary on the left side of the main altar when I went to daily Mass. In her long, flowing blue robes and soft, blond hair encircled by a halo of stars, Mary looked out at me as she held the baby Jesus. Sometimes I was sure that she winked. For me, she was the sacred image of the divine; I couldn't relate to God as father or as son. Like many people who have worshipped her throughout the ages, I brought Mary my childhood troubles and prayed for her comfort. She was the mother I yearned for. But I abandoned that outward form of devotion when I left the practice of Catholicism in my early twenties.

In my forties I began to long for her and I started to dream about a dark-skinned Madonna. I didn't know who she was; in fact, at the time, I had no knowledge of a "Black" Madonna. For me, the dream figure symbolized the dark unconscious I was delving into in therapy, reading about in ancient mythology and exploring in my photography. My dark dream woman appeared in many different forms: a mother cradling a child, a woman holding aloft a chalice, an old grandmother holding a Native American prayer pipe and teaching me how to pray.

At the time, and quite unrelated, I constructed a black-and-white abstract photographic montage of glacial ice for my friend

Linda, who lives in Alaska. When I presented it to her for her fiftieth birthday, she looked at it closely and said, "Oh, that's the Black Madonna of Le Puy." To me it looked like a crystal brain, but Linda went into her bedroom and brought out a small statue of the Le Puy Virgin she bought on pilgrimage in France. I immediately saw the resemblance. Linda was delighted that she could introduce me to her Madonna, so she immediately called her friend Susi in Switzerland and asked her to take me to see the Virgin of Le Puy next time I was in France.

Linda's naming of this image prompted my train ride three summers ago from Zurich to Einsiedeln and a subsequent plane ride to Marseilles to meet Susi and drive to Le Puy. There, after climbing hundreds of steps to the cathedral, I met the woman of my dreams. Her statue is small but her presence is huge. The *Vierge Noire* of Le Puy is a dark wood mother and child barely lit at night by one hanging lantern. When I saw her, I immediately began to cry.

I felt a stirring at my core of what I can only imagine the man at Einsiedeln must have felt when he pleaded with the dark-skinned mother. Hunger. I began to feel my own spiritual hunger. I do not know whether I would have recognized it as such had my own mother not passed on. But the child within me connected with the womb of the dark mother and all I longed for at that moment was her solace and embrace.

In her spiritual memoir, *Circling to the Center,* Geneva-based American-born writer Susan Tiberghien writes about discovering the Black Madonna of the Voirons in the dark woods outside

Geneva. I was very touched by her account, because it mirrored my own very visceral experience.

> I went for a walk in the woods on the side of the mountain overlooking the Lake of Geneva. I followed a narrow path, overrun with roots and stones, holding my thoughts—and myself—as still as possible. The path went deep into the dark trees before coming to a clearing, where there was an abandoned chapel. I pushed open the heavy door. In front of me, on a small wooden shelf in the stone wall behind the altar, stood a dark Madonna and child. . . . She was waiting there for me alone.
>
> I entered into her womb of darkness with my longings and my sorrows. I stood there, now a grandmother, carrying my family in my heart. I knew what the act of birth involves. I knew the dying to oneself that tears open the womb as the child is born. I had suffered this for each one of our children, feeling in my depths that this new life in my womb was too big for both it and me to survive. . . . Now it was Mary, the Mother of God, waiting to give birth to the child within me. Within her womb, I connected anew with the core of my being. For an instant of eternity, I experienced oneness— with God and with all of creation.

My own experience of the Black Madonna was not unlike Tiberghien's. For me, she embodies uncompromising compassion. I have sat, at different times, with both the Dalai Lama and Thich Nhat Hanh, and the compassion they embody is akin to the presence of the Black Madonna. I feel accepted to the very core of my being in her presence. She is a wellspring of support, reflection and containment.

Dark images of the divine mother have a long tradition in Eastern religions and in European and Central American Catholicism. Although there are over four hundred Black Madonnas throughout the world, they are relatively unknown and misunderstood. The Black Madonna, with her dark, unconscious, mysterious nature, is the embodiment of the feminine face of God. Thousands of pilgrims flock to her daily in her many sites throughout the world for solace and support. Her groundedness reflects us back to ourselves.

The Black Madonna has not been prettified; through the centuries she has denied patriarchal sentimentality. With her uncompromising gaze, she asks us to remain fully conscious. She accompanies us on the next step of our journey so that we become mindful of our lives. Because of her darkness, she absorbs us just as we are.

Root Memories

I've been a foreigner for the past twenty years. I don't have roots anymore. My roots are in my memory and my writing. That's why memory is so important. Who are you but what you can remember?

—Isabel Allende, *Poets and Writers* Magazine

I think of a root memory as a remembrance of something familiar that arouses a glimmer of recognition, perhaps something I have forgotten that remains just below the surface of my consciousness and emerges from time to time. The fact that a root memory is hidden does not mean that it is not active. Like a dream image, it informs us of who we are and who we might become. Certain powerful memories connect us to our culture, environment or bloodline and form the very fiber of our being. These roots remind us of our destiny.

When I was a child, every day after school, I would walk home down the long hill to the woods that bordered Hohokus Brook. There I would slip down the embankment under the bridge and enter my own private refuge, a secret world of matted leaves and overgrown trees, squirrels scurrying back and forth from limb to limb, fallen tree trunks bridging the water, blue jays and robins squawking at each other.

When I was sure that no one had followed me, I would hike back to my favorite tree bridge, shimmy out over the brook and look down. What fascinated me was how slowly the leaves swirled and floated to the rhythm of the water skimming the beautiful gray and blue pebbles underneath. Some leaves got caught, but others escaped. I would sit there mesmerized for what seemed like hours as the light and seasons changed. When the wail of the Erie Lackawanna in the distance signaled the arrival of commuters from the city, it was time for me to head home.

The rough tree bark against my thighs, the smell of autumn leaves and the flickering light on the brook were my companions. They rooted me in some way to my deeper nature away from the masks I wore at home and school. They provided a safe haven where I didn't have to live up to anyone's expectations. They still do. When I walk in the woods now with the trees forming a leafy multihued canopy, I feel like I am crossing a threshold into a remembered world of connection and freedom.

The woods became a touchstone for me. My memory of walking in them every day delights me now and, in some ways, defined me then. I have always wanted to live surrounded by nature, and I feel out of sorts when I am separated from tall, deciduous trees for any period of time. When we first moved to Los Angeles, I told my husband my body hurt because there was too much concrete. He told me I was crazy, but I had no other way to describe how I felt. My body ached because I missed the nurturing embrace of trees.

Perhaps it is this sense of place that Kathleen Norris writes about when she describes our quest for the sacred. For many of us, a particular landscape, a personal connection to nature or a relationship with a loved one or animal evokes a root memory, that of our first connection to "mother." Mother . . . *mater* . . . matter . . . earth. The memory of her heartbeat, her warmth, her voice, the rhythm of her body.

We may not actually know where memory originates, but we do know that infants recognize their mothers by smell. An infant's memory of mother is inextricably linked to the smell of her milk. So perhaps a root memory is that of an early smell, taste, sound, vision or texture of some person, place or thing that mysteriously signals who we will become. Perhaps that memory roots us in ourselves.

Blessed by Thunder

For Cuban-American memoirist Flor Fernandez Barrios, that root memory was planted by her grandmother Patricia in Cuba. The story her grandmother told Fernandez Barrios about her dramatic birth carried such intensity that it revealed her connection not only to the land of her origins, but to the line of women whose practice as healers would become her destiny.

Fernandez Barrios was born in the town of Cabaigüán in the middle of a hurricane. Just as she made her entrance into the world, a few minutes past midnight, a thunderbolt struck a pole nearby with such force that all the lights in the hospital went out. The delivery turned difficult as Fernandez Barrios's young mother screamed in pain and the doctor groped in the dark. Her grandmother Patricia, the local *curandera* present for the birth, started to pray aloud and the doctor silenced her. But she prayed anyway. She felt a strong presence in the hospital room, and when she looked away from her daughter-in-law struggling to give birth, she saw Santa Teresa de Avila, who reassured her that mother and child would be safe. The baby was subsequently named Flor Teresa for the saint.

In Fernandez Barrios's memoir, *Blessed by Thunder,* Grandmother Patricia tells her granddaughter this story to express her belief that the presence of thunder and the appearance of the saint at her birth are signs of her destiny to be a *curandera,* a healer. The old woman spends endless hours instructing her young granddaughter in the mysteries of life, from its most mundane aspects, such as how to clean the ceramic kitchen floor, to the serious subjects of spirituality and healing. But she doesn't tell the author about the destiny she sees for her until she is fourteen, the night before she and her family leave Cuba forever.

> "My mother was a yerbera," Grandmother Patricia said. "She was the kind of curandera who worked with herbs and plants to help people heal. My mother taught me what she knew and the night you were born, I knew you had been chosen by the spirit to be my apprentice. I knew it the second that lightning illuminated the sky. The healing power God has given me is like the energy of thunder. That's my don, my gift. You have it, too, Teresa! Someday you will be called to learn about this don, and it will be important for you to hear the call."

Over the years, Fernandez Barrios had witnessed her grandmother's healing power with people who had come from all over the island, yet the force of her grandmother's words startles her. She asks her what will happen if she does not hear the call. Her grandmother dismisses her fears: "'Don't you ever forget, you have been blessed by thunder. No matter where you go, you must remember my words!'"

Barrios and her family leave Cuba for "*El Norte*" and it is eight years before she sees her grandmother again. In her struggle to assimilate into a new culture, Fernandez Barrios forgets about her destiny. In spite of her loneliness and longing for the land of her birth, she works hard to put herself through college and prepares herself for medical school. When Grandmother Patricia comes to visit the family in Los Angeles, she reminds Fernandez Barrios of her healing rituals and the spirits that work with her.

"This tree," she said, pointing at the avocado, "is going to help you all heal the painful wounds from leaving Cuba. Your souls were shattered by the separation. Yesterday, when you and I were sitting next to the window, I was told by the spirits that it is okay to use the body of this tree to heal that pain."

"What spirits?" I interrupted.

"Spirits. Wise spirits who talk to me all the time."

"Tell me about them."

"There is not a whole lot to say. Spirits are spirits. They come and go in between the worlds. They talk to us. They breathe the same air we breathe, and they live with us. Some people see them with their eyes. Others feel the touch of these beings on their skin. Some simply hear their voices as clearly as you're hearing me."

"Grandmother, I know what you're talking about. I'm not sure, though, that I remember how to connect with them."

It would be years before Fernandez Barrios remembered how to connect with the spirit world of her childhood, but the unseen forces and ancient wisdom of her lineage were there waiting for her to explore when she was ready. Later, she had a powerful dream in which she was guided to leave traditional Western medicine to explore alternative healing practices. Making a wrenching decision to give up her Western persona, she entered graduate school to become a psychologist. Afterward, she studied with a Brazilian *curandera* and prepared her own altar and healing room to perform the ceremonies her grandmother had taught her.

In the end, it didn't matter how many years and miles separated Fernandez Barrios from her grandmother; time and distance collapsed. She never truly forgot the root of her destiny; her ancestral healing practices were just below her consciousness waiting to surface. The memory of her grandmother's story about her birth became the taproot that connects her to her past, nourishes her present and sustains her future. We never know what meaning an event has until it is revealed later.

Artifacts of Memory

I recently asked the students in my memoir class to write about an artifact or object. Rachel chose the loom she wove upon in the 1960s, when she and her husband lived in an intentional community, raising sheep, spinning and dyeing wool and making blankets, wall hangings and artsy coats. They moved around the country as their lives and work changed, but Rachel always set up the loom wherever they went. It was a viable presence everywhere they lived. She owned it for years before her mother commented upon it. One day, however, while visiting her in West Virginia, Rachel's mother ran her hand over the warp.

"You know, I used to do this in the camp," she said. "This was my job, to operate a weaving machine, in Czecho-slovakia. I would stand all day and make sure the—what do you call this thing?"

"The shuttle."

"The shuttle, is that what you call it? I don't remember what they called it in German, it'll come to me. I would stand all day and make sure that shuttle thing didn't get tangled in the—what do you call this?"

"The warp."

"Yes, the warp. I think it's the same in German. Make sure the shuttle didn't get tangled in the warp, because you know how sometimes if it doesn't go in straight, or it pulls too tight or not tight enough—"

"Yeah, I know that's the hard part. Getting it straight, with just the right amount of tension. It's where the craft is, the skill. The Navajos say they can tell the moment where you were distracted by looking at the edges of the weft."

Rachel had listened to many of her mother's stories about her years in the concentration camp before, but she didn't know until that day that her mother had worked a loom there. She had thought she was the first weaver in the family. Her mother stood in her living room staring down at the tangled threads, a blank look on her face, lost in her own reverie. Touching this familiar object had released a memory that had been locked away for decades.

Writing the memoir helped Rachel understand why her mother had never asked her about her weaving. She had not been able to separate her daughter's artistry from the memory of her own experience as a prisoner. It had just been too painful. The connection Rachel and her mother made that day over the loom dissolved years of seeming indifference and healed the uneasy silence between them.

Imprints of Memory

It was not until her eleven-year-old red-haired son started having seizures as a result of surgical trauma to his brain that another student, Jackie, recalled an early memory. When she was six, Jackie witnessed a red-haired mailman having an epileptic seizure on the sidewalk in the bright sun near her grandmother's house. His body jerked around in wild motions, and he emitted a strange, loud moaning. When she asked her mother what was wrong with the man, her mother said he was having a "fit" and hurried Jackie away. Looking back at the blue-clad figure with his bright orange hair on the dark asphalt, she was worried about him and had a premonition that she would visit this experience sometime in the future.

At fourteen, while having a snack at a drugstore counter with her girlfriends, she became aware of strange sounds and movements emanating from the young man sitting next to her. She knew something was wrong, so she moved her things to the other side of the U-shaped counter, where she guiltily watched the drama unfold.

The young man was having a seizure. A woman sitting on the other side of him was holding his body in her arms, trying to protect him, trying to still the spasms. Somehow I knew she was his mother—a rather gaunt woman wearing a black coat, her mottled gray hair pulled back in a knot. I can't remember what he looked like, only the woman holding him to her and the sad, worried expression on her face.

Jackie wondered why he was making those strange, frightening sounds, blowing bubbles of saliva out of his mouth. When her own son started having seizures, she recalled that day at the drugstore counter as well as the earlier seizure of the mailman on the asphalt: "Perhaps something happens that makes us think: Wait a minute, I've been here before. What was it? Oh, yes, that time when I was a child—*now* I know why I could never forget that scene." There is a strong element of recognition in a present experience that triggers a memory, conscious or not.

Medication controlled her young son's seizures reasonably well, but as an adult he suffers seizures without Jackie's embrace in restaurants, on buses, on streets, at work, in the gym. No longer living at home, it is usually the face of a stranger he encounters when consciousness returns.

Yet I have been that woman. I have cradled my son's body in my arms, shielding his head before gently lowering him to the floor while waiting for the spasms to ease, the guttural moans to subside, wiping away the saliva as it gurgles from his mouth. The fallen mailman, the protective mother, were they there to lead the way, to reassure me, to say, "You are not alone; this, too, can be endured"?

She wonders if certain memories may be mystical forewarnings, fleeting moments when all the tenses of our lives—past, present and future—merge together in one transcendental whole. Perhaps this is what a root memory provides, a window to the future.

Yesterday I saw my mother's shadow preceding me into the hospital. I was hurrying to see my friend David, who had just undergone open-heart surgery, and there was my mother's short, squat body rushing in ahead of me. My mother was always on the run; whether she was running from her life or running to her final destination, I don't know, but she didn't slow down until she began to lose her physical and mental faculties. The simpler her life became as Alzheimer's claimed her mind, the more she relaxed into it. Surrendering her temporal struggle, I believe she approached the nature of her true spirit.

But what shocked me yesterday as I looked at the shadow on the ground was how much my body has taken on her shape around the middle. In the past, my shadow always displayed my slim waist, but this image showed little differentiation between upper torso and hips. Not quite a fireplug or sausage, but certainly not an hourglass either.

Now when I look in the mirror at my reflection, my face seems to take on more and more of my mother's characteristics. The wrinkles on the left side of my mouth extend from the corner of my smile down to my jaw. The deep crevice growing there was her mother's and then hers. I always wondered, as a child, why they wrinkled vertically instead of horizontally. Now I know, the wrinkles just appear there. No amount of Lancôme's Rénergie seems to fluff up the flesh.

As she approached eighty, my mother planted an English garden of pale yellow columbines, bluebells, delphiniums and spidery ferns. There was a sparseness and fragility to this dew-soaked lacy tapestry, so unlike the hearty rhododendrons my father planted beside it. It was her last attempt to stake out her plot on this earth. She wanted life to be simple; she wanted to look out the window each day and watch the delicate flowers bloom and the hummingbirds sip at her feeder.

The essence of memoir is to accompany the writer as she struggles to make meaning from her life. What we don't understand about the mysteries of our life is as good a place to start exploring as the things we do know and comprehend. When I first started to write about my relationship with my mother, I was aware that revisiting certain memories would be difficult, yet I was curious where the process would take me. I originally wanted not only to penetrate the source of our fission, but also to understand how memory tempers identity. What we remember from our past contains the clues to our present and future. A well-written memoir holds the pattern that memory reveals of our life.

Did I ever come to know my mother? Probably not; I don't

think we ever come to truly know another person, but I did come to appreciate her struggle and to love her. Is that because she could no longer hurt me? Certainly. When she was a younger woman she could say cruel things. When my first husband and I decided to separate, she roared, "Look at this house! No Beverly Hills lawyer would ever want to live here!" On the contrary, our Venice Beach bungalow was actually quite wonderful, clean and homey; my husband and I both loved it. The house was not the problem; it had nothing to do with our decision to separate. But I had disappointed her yet again.

In contrast, the last time she was lucid before she died, she said to me, "Don't you look pretty." Who knows if she actually recognized me, but I cherished her warmth that day. I came to an acceptance of who she was as she faded away; now I see her taking form within me.

Last month while walking in the woods in upstate New York, I heard my mother's voice whispering in the trees. "Slow down, you don't have to work so hard anymore." The sound of her voice startled me, as did the sentiment, but I wasn't surprised that it was in the woods that I could hear her. I had to go back to my roots to truly listen.

She reminds me not to lose connection with the natural world and the wonder before it I experienced as a child. In many ways, the woods became my mother, but the essence of the woman's nature, along with her wrinkles and shape, will live on within me.

PART TWO

On Writing Memoir

Why Write Memoir?

I've taken the memoir route on the ground that even an idling memory is apt to get right what matters most. I used to say, proudly, that I would never write a memoir, since "I am not my own subject." Now I'm not so sure. After all, one's recollected life is just about all that's left at the end of the day when the work is done and gone, property now of others.

—Gore Vidal, *Palimpsest*

*I*f you've gotten this far in this book, you must be thinking about writing your own memoir. But then you begin to worry, "Who would be interested in me? I'm not famous, I'm not a celebrity; I've led a rather small life." But if you take that thought a little bit further, you'd realize that your singular life may also reflect, in an important way, the lives of other men and women of your particular age, race, sexual orientation or culture. As you attempt to know yourself better, you provide your readers with insight into their own lives. The secret is to tell your particular life story so that it adds to our collective understanding of what it is to be human.

People write memoir for many reasons. Some write to discover their old story, to recover what was lost, to touch it once again, to put it on record. Others use memoir to find the true self—hidden beneath public persona of ambition, success, heartache or failure. Still others write to bear witness to their life—I lived, I loved, I experienced loss and I yearned just like you. Some writers explore memoir to lay the family demons to rest, to let them go once and for all, so that they may fully live their present "story." Others write memoir to heal a relationship, to come to terms with an illness, to find community. But more often than not, people write memoir because their story just must be told.

My personal impulse in writing memoir has been to understand—to genuinely inquire about certain events in my life so that I can recognize the continuing influence of these defining moments and move beyond them. My struggles with my mother throughout my life had an enormous influence on how I developed as a woman. In writing my memoir in Part One, I wanted to understand how her loss of identity through her loss of memory affected our relationship and ultimately led to our healing. Because I am a psychotherapist, I had previously thought of this as a primarily psychological process, because I am interested in making the unconscious themes and images in my life conscious. But in writing my memoir and reflecting upon the compassion and forgiveness we touched in each other, I found the writing itself transformational.

Self-reflection and insight are essential to transformation. Memoirs that are solely confessional in tone and content do not transform. The self-reflection required of memoir writing prepares the way for the evolution of a new self. We are, after all, the only species we know of that reflects upon its memories.

When we write a story about a particular memory—for example, in my case the five-year-old who wanted to know how to draw a tree or the seventeen-year-old who heard a voice in the chapel—the event loses its hold on us. It no longer has us by the nape of the neck reminding us how to *think* or *feel* about ourselves as we might have thought or felt about ourselves at the time the event occurred.

In writing the piece about hearing the voice in the chapel, turning around and leaving my childhood vocation in the last pew, I have been able to accept that my life has evolved in its own order and divine plan. In other words, I have been able to let go—of all of the expectations and guilt attached to that event. It helps, of course, to have some distance from which to reflect upon it. If I had written this piece right after walking away from the novitiate, going home and seeing my mother cry, it would be a very different memoir. It was the writing of the memory at this point in my life that allowed the transformation.

A transformation in the way a writer views her world is not uncommon to the memoir process. In the first chapter of *In My Mother's House,* Kim Chernin's memoir about her mother, a strong personality and Communist organizer active in the first half of the twentieth century in New York, the author admits to the immense resistance she felt to her mother's pressure to write her life story. Chernin is afraid of losing her own life as a poet in the process.

> I am torn by contradiction. I love this woman. She was my first great aching love. All my life I have wanted to do whatever she asked of me, in spite of our quarreling.
>
> She is old, I say to myself. What will it take from you? Give this to her. She's never asked anything from you as a writer before. Give this. You can always go back to your own work later.
>
> But it is not so easy to turn from the path I have imagined for myself. This enterprise will take years. It will draw me

back into the family, waking its ghosts. It will bring the two of us together to face all the secrets and silences we have kept. The very idea of it changes me. I'm afraid. I fear, as any daughter would, losing myself back into the mother.

What happened instead was that in the seven years it took Chernin to write the lives of her mother, grandmother, daughter and self, she became *more* of herself, not less. In her perennial struggle to differentiate herself from her mother she had not realized how much she had lost in rejecting one aspect of her mother, that was at the core of her own being, a Jewish woman. She had cast aside her mother's dogma and it broke her mother's heart. When she finished the book, her mother spoke to her in a voice she had never heard before, which Chernin acknowledged as pure feeling: "I love you more than life, my daughter. I love you more than life."

Geoffrey Wolff too finds deep compassion and acceptance for his father (and himself) by the final chapter of his memoir, *The Duke of Deception*, although in the opening chapter he admits to uttering "Thank God" when he learns his father is dead. Perhaps writing memoir does have the ability to transform the writer. In finding the moment of memory that stands as a metaphor for a part—or the whole—of a relationship, the writer is capable of moving beyond the old image and being healed.

Memoir and Community

Memoir writing is not merely an individual self-reflective act. Yes, the writer reflects upon her own life experience, but in doing so, she trusts that the reader will find meaning in her life as well. My hope is that as you read about the tumult in my relationship with my mother and our ultimate healing, you will find solace too. An individual memory becomes the repository of a family or cultural memory. In writing memoir and trusting that our stories have value, we gain access to the larger culture. Passing our life story on to the next generation preserves the culture. In writing the secrets that have not been said aloud but must not be forgotten, we honor the struggles and dignity of our people.

Novelist Amy Tan has collected her mother's stories not only to inform the characters in her novels, but also to help her mother transform the ghosts of her past. Tan is quoted in the *New York Times Book Review* as saying about her mother, "She wanted someone to go back and relive her life with her. It was a way for her to exorcise her demons, and for me to finally listen and empathize and learn what memory means, and what you can change about the past."

A memoir is not simply about the writer; it is also about anyone who has touched her life and the relationship they have shared. The memoir writer also creates community with the reader, as together they develop understanding and empathy as they each make meaning of the memory. In addition, writing memoir as part of a writing group provides the support some writers need to explore and change the past.

I have led one women's memoir group for the last six years. The writers react differently to producing assigned writing on a regular basis, but they agree that the trust they have developed together as they reflect upon and shape their lives has had an enormous impact on their writing. Writing is easier for some people to do in community; they feel supported by the collective creativity and camaraderie.

You may also find that writing in a group helps you keep a regular writing schedule. If you gather a group of writers together to meet on a weekly or monthly basis, you may be more likely to produce work. Some groups write for twenty to thirty minutes during the time they are together and then read their work aloud and ask for constructive comments. Other groups prepare work in advance and bring copies to the group members to be read aloud. Many groups combine both approaches. Your writing group need not be large; starting with five writers is enough. You can rotate leaders to keep time or hire a teacher to help you get started.

Reading work aloud in a group provides both comfort and risk: comfort in the support of others and risk in exposing one's vulnerability. One member of our group, Hillary, comments:

> Memoir writing pushes me out of my comfort zone. In this wildly different group of women, we have opened up chapters of our lives that we have shared with no one else. The safe and nurturing environment created by these women allows me to read aloud material I have wept over my computer writing. When you feel people will catch you with kind hands, it makes it easier to run and jump into unknown terrain.

Our Irish writer, Bairbre, agrees:

> We had one man in our class at UCLA, a Zen practitioner

who was in a rock band in the sixties. He didn't opt to join us when we reconfigured at Maureen's house. Imagine what it must be like to listen to women and not try to fix their lives, their direction, their sadness. Just to listen and be listened to, hearing yourself and others. Imagine going through life thinking that everything you did was enough, was right, was even fabulous. Well, we did this. We wrote, we unfolded, we blossomed.

Bairbre makes a point about women's memoir that is important. Many women never feel that what they've done in their lives, what they've given, is enough. The act of writing their life changes that. They begin to view themselves not only through their struggles or through the lens of mother, wife, daughter, sister, friend or worker, but they begin to stake a larger claim for themselves in the world, as potent agents of their destiny. I live, I think, I have dreams, I am. They discover a core sense of self.

I recently received a letter from one of my septuagenarian writing students calling our memoir group her "lifeline." That term, "lifeline," impressed me. Having sailed in Nova Scotia, I know what it is like to be attached to a lifeline in rough seas, and I also know how indispensable it is. Without a lifeline, you may quickly perish. When I commented upon her use of the word, Jackie said, "I meant it; this memoir group gives me a connection I would not otherwise have to my life. I have made self-discoveries here, sometimes painful, sometimes cathartic. I feel like I'm doing something."

Carolyn Heilbrun agrees; in *Hamlet's Mother and Other Women* she writes, "Pain is not easier for having been suffered before in the same way, but it is more bearable for having been narrated." We close our eyes and hear an echo to our story.

What distinguishes memoir from any other genre is just that echo. When you write your memoir you will understand, perhaps for the first time, the significance of your life through the language, images and emotions you craft from the memory. Whether you write to recover what was lost, heal a relationship, discover a secret, come to terms with an illness or chronicle an adventure, when you write your memoir and read it aloud to another, you will hear your own truth. And truth transforms.

Getting Started

Rather than simply telling a story from her life, the memoirist both tells the story and muses upon it, trying to unravel what it means in the light of her current knowledge. The contemporary memoir includes retrospection as an essential part of the story. Your reader has to be willing to be both entertained by the story itself and interested in how you now, looking back on it, understand it.

—Judith Barrington, *Writing the Memoir*

A memoir is how a writer remembers the events of her life, chronicling the journey from "there to here." But rather than simply recounting an incident or a memory from her life, the memoirist both tells the story and tries to make meaning out of it.

The memoir presupposes that there is a certain unity to human experience, that we all share similar hopes, dreams and desires. When a writer recounts a memory about herself, she is talking about all of us to some degree. The essence of memoir is to participate in the writer's struggle to achieve some understanding of the events, traumas and triumphs of her personal recollection. For a piece of writing to be called a memoir it must include self-reflection. Without it, the recollection of an incident or incidents lacks depth and cannot lead to transformation. Like any good piece of writing, memoir must affect our experience of what it is to be human.

When we tell our story and tell it well, in a way that reflects the universal experience of being human, we become a part of each other. Memoir is not autobiography—a recounting of linear events from birth to death—but rather a *selected* aspect of a life. How the writer selects that aspect is crucial to the success of her piece. The writer has to know—not necessarily right away, but at some point—what it is she really wants to write about, which in turn will tell her what to leave out. *Being willing to leave things out is vital.* Writing is ultimately about making choices.

As you begin to write your memoir, bear in mind the following elements found in most memoirs: remembered event, universal theme, relational style, emotional truth, intimacy, humor and self-reflection. When you read published memoirs, begin to notice the distinct elements they feature.

Remembered Event

No event is too small or too insignificant to write about. That's the beauty of memoir writing—it's *how* you write your story that matters. One should choose a memory that has value, one that others might find interesting. Is there some discovery you'd like to make about a particular life event, some coincidence, some anecdote from your life that would interest other people, some challenge you've met, some crisis you've survived, some secret you've uncovered or some actual life occurrence stranger than fiction?

Remember, a memoir is not simply a factual retelling of your life: This happened, then that happened and then that. This type of travelogue eventually becomes flat and boring. There has to be something unique about the event you remember that will keep the reader interested.

However, this doesn't mean the event itself must be unusual. We all have events in our lives that seem mundane to us but are unique to the reader. For example, in *Episodes,* Pierre Delattre's series of vignettes about his life, the author writes a short piece about hiding in the laundry chute at age nine while playing hide-and-seek with his older brother: "I opened the wooden door to the clothes chute, backed my rump into it, bent forward, and sat on a pile of sheets. Then I raised up and, wiggling my way to a standing position inside, pulled the door closed with the toe of my shoe."

Delattre sets the environment and invites the reader into his memory using a very detailed explanation of his movement. One can envision exactly how and where he hid, because many of us have hidden in secret places as children.

Once Delattre finds his bearings, he discovers that this particular laundry chute is a distinctive enclosure: The door opens only from the outside. Once he closes the door, he cannot escape until his brother finds him: "I heard it click shut and found myself standing there in the dark. I panicked. What if I couldn't get the door open? I kicked off one of my shoes and felt with my stockinged toe for a latch. There was none."

As a reader, I can empathize with his panic, because all of a sudden, I become a nine-year-old trapped in a small dark space. Most young children share this universal fear of being left in a dark, unfamiliar place. Delattre uses a remembered event that most readers can relate to whether they have had the same experience as a child or not. We all fear being lost in the dark.

The other feature of this laundry chute that Delattre describes is the fact that the chute goes straight up to a little door in the back wall of his parents' bedroom. And his parents are asleep. Or so the author thought. "I was anxious about what would happen to me when my father found out that I had hidden in a strictly forbidden place, especially when he had made it clear so many times that I shouldn't interrupt his and my mom's naps for any reason whatsoever." As soon as we read that sentence, we know that the author's childhood world, as he has known it, is about to change.

Delattre's memoir is not just about playing hide-and-seek with his older brother, or climbing into a laundry chute. His reminiscence about innocent childhood games leads to a revelation, and the author's humorous recounting of being sequestered in the dark becomes a memoir about sexual awakening.

Memoirs of childhood illustrate the fact that seeds planted in our youth have enormous impact on who we become as adults. When we read about a writer's childhood, we too remember the innocence we felt when life was not as compartmentalized as it is now and "play" really meant time to daydream, explore, observe nature, have adventures, eat hot dogs and watermelon and hang out with friends. A friendlier time, a more spacious time. A time to relax, observe others, feel the grass under our bare feet, fall in love.

In William Zinsser's *Inventing the Truth,* memoirist Annie Dillard discusses the feelings she revisited in *An American Childhood*: "A child wakes up over and over again, and notices that she's living. A child dreams along, loving the exuberant life of the senses, in love with beauty and power, oblivious of herself, and then suddenly, bingo, she wakes up and feels herself alive."

Because time is more spacious in childhood, or perhaps because a child is closer to the ground and the world is a brand-new frontier, many memoirs of childhood are rich in sensual details. The writer's memory of smells, tastes, colors, textures and sounds is vivid. Whenever I give students the assignment to write a first childhood memory or, specifically, their memory of their first lunchtime at school, the details amaze me. How can anyone in her thirties, forties or fifties remember the exact sensation associated with her first taste of brown sugar sandwiches when she was six, or the smell of peanut butter and jelly sandwiches when she was five?

The answer is that those initial sense experiences remain distinct. What we see, hear, taste, smell, touch and observe in childhood sticks. Remembering the house she loved as a child, memoirist Alice Kaplan writes: "I loved to hide in that house. I hid under the grand piano, to watch the argyle socks of my sister's dates. I crouched on the staircase, to watch my parents' parties. I hid behind the couch. Everyone had an activity I wanted to observe."

The sensory experience of childhood is encountered once again in the details the memoirist chooses to include. Kaplan remembers the *argyle* socks of her sister's dates as she hid beneath the grand piano, and Delattre tries to open the latch of that dark laundry chute with his *stockinged* foot. We can almost feel that stubborn latch with our own toes. When I wrote about my tree-drawing incident, the image that brought the memory back to me was that of my father's multihued Prismacolor pencils, which I always coveted.

The writer does not need to provide every detail of the remembered event, just the details that matter. As Delattre's account unfolds, his mother opens the laundry chute above and releases her panties. Delattre's description of his mother's panties landing on his forehead is riveting:

> They slid over my eyes, nose, and chin. I was smothered for a moment by an aroma of wilted roses. The panties dropped to my feet. I got my other shoe off and felt around with my stockinged feet until I was able to step into the leg holes of the panties.

When you begin to write your remembered event, remember to include sensory details. Delattre uses kinesthetic sensation, smell and emotion. A master at choosing just the right details, he is more successful evoking mood and tension with selected sense memories than are many writers who try to describe their feelings. After writing about a particular incident, look carefully at your work and ask yourself, "Is this particular detail important to my understanding of this event? To the reader's? Does it add emotional truth? How will the piece work without it?" Remember that a few carefully chosen words can often convey great meaning.

Your memory may be dim at first, but it will become clearer with exercise. Writers often lament, "I can't remember all the details of what happened. It was so many years ago." That's okay, you don't have to remember all the details. Your memory of an event or a particular time in your life may be nothing more than a fleeting image at first. Start with that image, whatever it is, and follow it. It may be nothing more than the corner of the room, a chair, the sound of your mother's voice. It's a starting place, like the beginning of any journey.

In discussing her own remembering process, Toni Morrison

writes, "The image comes first and tells me what the 'memory' is about." She is referring to her recollection of the sound of her mother's voice when she and her friends traded gossip around the kitchen table about a particular woman in their small town. The tone of her mother's voice changed. It carried a certain "knowing" tone that informed Morrison that the woman had broken some taboo and become an outcast. That sound memory led to the creation of the title character in Morrison's novel *Sula*.

Your memory image might be the smell of lilacs in early spring or the taste of warm toast, the way your mother's hair fell down the back of her neck as she cooked in summer, the angry color of your newborn brother's cheeks when he hollered, the sweat on your father's brow, the soft texture of your puppy's fur or a movement of your bedroom curtain in the breeze at night when you were alone.

In "The Table," Alyce Miller chose her mother's living-room end table as a memoir topic because the table contained a puzzle she could not resist as a young girl. Her mother had received the table on her wedding day as a present from a furniture-maker friend of her father. Attached to its underside was an envelope with the instruction that it could not be opened for one hundred years. The contents of the envelope became a great source of curiosity for Miller, and she would lie under the table for hours puzzling about what was written inside.

Lying there, staring up, I was made crazy by the possibilities. I did my very best to penetrate the contents of the envelope with focused concentration. The table maker's instructions rang in my head like the interdiction from a fairy tale. *Don't go into the woods.*

Miller's memory evolves into a memoir about her relationship with her mother, their different personalities and opinions about keeping a promise. She explores how the passage of time affects one's guess-work about the unknown and how our lives intersect with the lives of others whom we will never meet. This rich reverie resulted from the simple act of staring up at the underside of a living-room end table.

Writing Suggestion

In order to choose a remembered event, start by writing down the first fifteen years of your life in fifteen minutes. Set a timer and write as quickly as possible; don't take your pen off the paper. This is called a "free write." Just write whatever comes to your mind in whatever order it appears. Don't worry at this point about punctuation or paragraphs. Just follow your pen, or if you are using a computer, follow your fingers. Don't censor and don't judge. Don't ask, "Did this really happen?" Assume that it did.

If you draw a blank on your childhood, recall a more recent decade, say, your thirties, forties or the last ten years of your life. Choose a time in your life that seems accessible; this exercise is just for priming the pump.

When you have finished, read what you have written aloud and pick one incident *you* want to learn more about. Circle it. You may have two or three events you'd like to explore, but for the purpose of this exercise, choose the one that holds the most interest for you. If you want to discover more about a particular memory, there's a good chance your reader will want to know more about it too. If none of these events appeal to you, select your first day at school. Most people have an emotional memory of the first day of school.

Now focus on the memory. What are the colors you remember, the sounds, the smells, the tastes, the textures, your feelings? What is unusual about this incident? What is novel? What is humorous?

Start with one image and use all your senses to reexperience it. Using the first day of school as an example, what shoes did you wear to school that day? What clothes? Where was your school? In the city, in the country, in the suburbs, at home? How did you get there? Did you walk, take the school bus, ride in a car pool? Was anyone with you? Did you take your lunch to school, or was a school lunch prepared for students? If you took your lunch to school, did you have a lunch box? What did it look like? What was inside? Where did you eat? Who did you sit with? Did you meet a friend? What were you afraid of?

In *The Color of Water*, James McBride writes poignantly about being teased by his brothers and sisters on his first day of school:

> I was terrified when it came my turn to go to school. Although P.S. 118 was only eight blocks away, I wasn't allowed to walk there with my siblings because kindergarten students were required to ride the bus. On the ill-fated morning, Mommy chased me all around the kitchen trying to dress me as my siblings laughed at my terror. "The bus isn't bad," one quipped, "except for the snakes. Sometimes the bus never brings you home." Guffaws all around.

McBride's reward for weathering his siblings' teasing was that his mother, with whom he never had any private time with eleven other siblings around, walked him alone to the bus stop. Recalling this incident forty years later, McBride captures the reader's imagination by presenting not only the image of him eluding his mother as she tries to get him dressed, but also the specter of snakes on the school bus. While you may not have anything as colorful as McBride to relate about your first day of school, you should notice that the author, like most skilled writers, makes good use of general storytelling devices: a description of character and place, an incident, dialogue, and tension or conflict. In doing so he helps us understand what it felt to be like him.

Now write that first memory with as much sensual detail as you can capture. After you recount the details of the memory and read what you have written, notice what the underlying story is. Is there tension in the story, a pivotal event? What is the emotional essence of your remembrance? What does this incident reveal about you or another person involved in the memory? Was dialogue exchanged? How did this incident resolve itself? Are there details that you have written that are unnecessary to the telling of your story? What do you now know about yourself that you didn't know before writing this piece?

Answering these questions will help you identify whether or not there is a sense of universality to this memory, or a theme to which the reader can relate. Note how McBride touches our universal fear of change, of embarking upon something that is totally unfamiliar. This resonance is critical to the success of memoir.

Universality

I want to record how the world comes at me, because I think it is indicative of the way it comes at everyone.

—Phillip Lopate, *The Art of the Personal Essay*

As I've mentioned before, memoir trades on the universality of memories, reflecting the dreams, desires and feelings we all share. Regardless of whether the specific facts of your life are different from mine, we can both relate to the excitement and longing involved in a first romance, the sense of wonder watching the first snowfall of the season, the disappointment experienced in being betrayed by a good friend, the sense of adventure in traveling to a new land or the grief and disbelief involved in the death of a loved one. The facts are individual, but the *feelings* are universal.

Reading about McBride's first day of school brought back all of my own trepidation about being in a schoolroom for the first time with fifty other children and Sister Evangeline. My heart actually started to race as I remembered kicking the nun in her shins under her long black habit as she tried to extricate me from my mother. If the writer searches for the emotional truth of her experience, the reader will be able to relate it to her memory too.

In addition to invoking universal feelings, memoirists also address universal themes: birth, love, loss, death, the journey. Delattre writes about childhood innocence and its loss; McBride writes about leaving home for the first time. Others deal with psychological, spiritual or healing journeys; adventures into the wilderness; rites of passage such as falling in love, marriage and betrayal; friendships found and friendships lost; initiation and descent; illness and recovery; midlife, aging, elderhood and the acceptance of death; the pursuit of community. One of the reasons that *Angela's Ashes* was so widely acclaimed was that it is a powerful account of the dignity and resilience of the human spirit in the face of abject poverty and oppression. Anyone who has experienced any form of oppression would be inspired by McCourt's compassion and humor in the face of terrible day-to-day living conditions in Ireland. He invites the reader into his heart, not to lament his woes, but to celebrate the endurance of his family.

Memoirs that are written to glorify one's victimhood, exalt one's triumphs, claim affiliation with someone famous or reveal the frailties or peccadilloes of another for revenge may contain archetypal tendencies we all share—that of victim, hero or avenger—but unless there is self-reflection and a search for meaning, the writing lacks the depth of universal truth that underlies our search for meaning. In *A Chorus of Stones,* poet Susan Griffin writes:

I am beginning to believe that we know everything, that all history, including the history of each family, is part of us, such that, when we hear any secret revealed, a secret about a grandfather, or an uncle, or a secret about the battle of Dresden in 1945, our lives are made suddenly clearer to us, as the unnatural heaviness of unspoken truth is dispersed. For perhaps we are like stones; our own history and the history of the world embedded in us, we hold a sorrow deep within and cannot weep until that history is sung.

I agree with Griffin that not only is our personal history embedded within us, but also the history of the world with its joys and sufferings.

Nuala O'Faolain was stunned by the universal response to her memoir, *Are You Somebody?* She admits that she wasn't thinking of her readers when she was writing the book; she was trying to make sense of growing up female in her particular circumstances in twentieth-century Ireland. But she struck a chord that went far beyond the details of her life. Her readers insisted on her seeing their lives reflected as well.

She received fan letters from Trinidad, Australia, China, Rome and even from a trekker's hut in Nepal. The writers offered her images of themselves in notes pushed through her door, in letters to the newspaper where she worked, in correspondence to her publisher. Hundreds of people wrote from "kitchens and bedrooms and fireside chairs where men and women unknown to me had sat all night—in a sense with me—reading me."

Her story, which she said she didn't think anyone would care about, gave meaning to the disparate events of her life. "I never envisaged such cherishing," she writes. "When I called my memoir *Are You Somebody?* it was largely to preempt the hostile people who'd say, at my writing anything about myself at all, 'Who does she think she is?' I never imagined awakening something a bit like love."

O'Faolain evoked such love perhaps because she writes with amazing honesty about her aloneness as a middle-aged woman. Most writers don't reveal something as vulnerable as their personal loneliness, for fear of being castigated, but O'Faolain's readers related to her words because they understood her feelings. In allowing others to see all of her rough spots, she holds up a mirror to anyone who dares to look at herself with courage, love and compassion.

Memoir deals with our personal experience as well as our opinions, attitudes and our most cherished feelings—at any age. It is a common human experience to have feelings and prejudices we don't want revealed, whether they are about race, gender, age, sexual preference or religious orientation. We don't want others to know how we feel, because we don't want to be rejected. So we—not only individuals, but whole groups of people—develop an internal censor for fear of revealing too much. Some memoirists however, use this genre to courageously explore the origin of these prejudices.

McBride wrote his memoir to explore his racial origins. His black stepfather died when McBride was fourteen years old, and his white mother, refusing to learn how to drive her husband's car, rode her blue bicycle everywhere in the black projects where they lived in Brooklyn. McBride shares his adolescent revulsion to her whiteness:

> The image of her riding that bicycle typified her whole existence to me. Her oddness, her complete non-awareness of what the world thought of her, a nonchalance in the face

of what I perceived to be imminent danger from blacks and whites who disliked her for being a white person in a black world.

Almost everyone can relate to the experience of being embarrassed, at some point, in some small way, by a parent's behavior. I was mortified, as a teenager, each time my mother sang out the hymns at Sunday Mass. She was so loud that everyone would turn to look at her and all I wanted to do was disappear under the pew.

Several contemporary memoirists have written eloquently about the universal feeling of longing, specifically about the longing for their father—to know him, to find him, to be separate from him. I have already mentioned Jenny Diski's longing for the ideal father in Danny Kaye. Mary Gordon explores who her father *really* was instead of whom he told her he was in *The Shadow Man,* and Germaine Greer searches over three continents for the father who never came back intact from World War II in *Daddy, We Hardly Knew You.* In *The Duke of Deception,* Geoffrey Wolff discovers that no matter how hard he tries to escape his father through geographical distance, education and professional success, the man lives on in his very cells. He concludes his memoir about the con artist who was his father by writing:

> I cannot now shake this conviction, that I was trained as his instrument of perpetuation, put here to put him into the record. And that my father knew this, calculated it to a degree. . . . Writing to a friend about this book, I said that I would not now for anything have had my father be other than what he was, except happier, and that most of the time

he was happy enough, cheered on by imaginary successes. He gave me a great deal, and not merely life, and I didn't want to bellyache; I wanted, I told my friend, to thumb my nose on his behalf at everyone who had limited him.

My friend was shrewd, though, and said that he didn't believe me, that I couldn't mean such a thing, that if I followed out its implications I would be led to a kind of ripe sentimentality, and to mere piety. Perhaps, he wrote me, you would not have wished him to lie to himself, to lie about being a Jew. Perhaps you would have him fool others but not so deeply trick himself. "In writing about a father," my friend wrote me about our fathers, "one clambers up a slippery mountain, carrying the balls of another in a bloody sack, and whether to eat them or worship them or bury them decently is never cleanly decided."

The paradoxical nature of the complex feelings we have for our father, whether we are male or female, is truly universal. Each one of us knows the deep longing we share for the man we call "father," whether he has been an active presence in our life or not. That's why we can relate to the loss experienced by each author; every singular death becomes universal.

Writing Suggestion

Look at the free write of the first fifteen years of your life from the last writing exercise and choose an incident that has a universal theme. For example, I have found that for most women, the memory of getting a first bra elicits myriad universal feelings: expectation, excitement, embarrassment, fear and humiliation. The story of one's first bra can also be hilarious.

In *Cherry,* Mary Karr writes about asking her daddy for money for her first bra one afternoon while they are shelling pecans. At eleven, she has to use both hands to squeeze the nutcracker, which sends shards flying all over the rug and leaves the pecans smushed. Her dad, amused by her request to buy a bra, takes the nutcracker from her hands and deftly cracks the shell, the husk falling into the bowl intact. But Karr doesn't want just a bra; she wants something more. Her thirteen-year-old sister Lecia already fills a 36-C cup.

> "What're you angling for, then, Pokey?" he asked.
> What I wanted formed in my head for a good instant before I said it. "I want titties, goddam it, Daddy." His eyes widened slowly at what I'd dared to say. "You want titties?"
> He threw back his head and hooted with laughter.

Karr powerfully portrays the universal comparison of self to other that is such an integral part of adolescence and sibling rivalry.

One of my writing students, Alice, wrote about her pride in being the first girl in sixth grade to wear a bra and her subsequent humiliation when the school principal gave her a vest to hide those same developing breasts.

That year, Alice was chosen to lead the school's annual Halloween procession. The day before the event, Sister Clemencia called Alice into her office and handed her a vest to wear over her school uniform. Alice was startled, confused and immediately sensed that there was more to this vest than Sister Clemencia was saying.

"Will the other girls be wearing this vest or just me?"

"Just you, Alice. We believe that you are too young to be wearing a bra. If you insist on keeping up this charade of thinking you are older than you actually are, then we insist you wear this vest whenever the weather is too hot for you to keep your sweater on."

Alice tried to hide her humiliation by imagining that the other six hundred students would covet her leadership position.

Perhaps you'd like to write about your first bra, a friendship, your first love, leaving home, your first job, getting married, giving birth. Choose an event from your life that carries a universal theme and write a story that is approximately seven hundred words long. I suggest seven hundred words because you can capture the emotional essence of a memory in a very few words. Experiment with dialogue and give as much detail as you can about your experience. Karr's description of using two hands to shell pecans while she is talking to her father gives us information about just how small she is. As you write, imagine that you are telling the story to a very close friend.

Intimacy, Relational Style and Tense

The longing to tell one's story and the process of telling is symbolically a gesture of longing to recover the past in such a way that one experiences both a sense of reunion and a sense of release.

— bell hooks, *Remembered Rapture*

The hallmark of memoir is its intimacy with its reader. The memoirist speaks directly into our ear, confiding everything from wisdom to gossip, relating internal dialogues and disputes. Memoirists are adept at letting the reader in on their personal queries. They ask the questions we all wish we had thought to ask and tell the stories we never thought we'd hear.

In discussing her memoir *Poets in Their Youth,* Eileen Simpson quotes poet Robert Lowell as saying that there is nothing so refreshing after a hard day's work as gossip. Repetition, like the sharing of gossip, deepens the memory groove. Writing a memoir is similar to sharing gossip; both stimulate recall. As we deepen the memory groove through the writing of an event, we find that the tale takes on new colors, textures and nuances.

The language of memoir is relational; the narrator is involved in a conversation with the reader. It is as if the writer sits down with a close friend over a cup of tea or a beer to tell an intimate story. She not only recounts what happened, but she also engages herself in the queries and reflections she might in fact address in dialogue with a close friend. She relates the essence of her story, her reactions and her insights.

Relational Style

When you choose an event and begin your first draft, write what it is that you wish to say directly and simply in short, clear sentences. No long-winded explanations are needed, but plenty of wit is welcome. The reader doesn't want an analysis of your life; she's interested in the drama of your story. She doesn't need to be told why an event is significant; the writing of it should gently lead her there.

What happened when you moved across the country to play college basketball and missed the winning three-point shot in the last second of the championship game? Where were you when you first fell in love? How did you get your first job? Who helped you dress on the day of your wedding? Memoir deals with everyday life events and what you make of them upon reflection.

One of my writing students, Brooke, is a runner and suffers with the challenges of diabetes. She recently wrote a memoir, "Stairclimb to the Top," about her footrace up fifteen hundred steps to the top of the Library Tower in Los Angeles. In her piece, Brooke describes the other runners and queries the reader and herself about who these people are who put themselves through such physical rigors. Written in present tense, she gives the reader a very intimate view of what a runner with fluctuating blood sugar levels must face each moment of a race. This particular component of running is one of which most of us would never be aware.

I exercise fervently for weeks before the big "Stair Climb." I am possessed. I tell no one why my schedule is so busy. Only my family know and they ignore my anxiety. I know I can climb to the top; I have done it before but can I do it this time? I ask the question a thousand times a day. The week of the event I stretch and breathe obsessively. I continue the stair practice. I time myself. I do ten round trips that equal eighty stories. I feel fat and stiff. My legs are not at all limber. They weigh me down. Nothing bends.

The night before the race I am extremely careful about what I eat. More cautious than usual. I need to have energy. I awaken at 3 A.M. with my heart pounding, a sure sign of low blood sugar. I pop two glucose tablets into my mouth, put a pillow over my head and try to think of nothingness.

Brooke's writing style invites the reader to join her in her climb. The tension builds on each step not only because of her subject matter, but also because of her sentence structure—her sentences are short and lean—her use of present tense and her confessional style.

The fog has lifted. Without thinking I look up to the top and instantly my body fills with fear. The building appears to be extraordinarily high. I cannot do this. I must do this. I feel like I am about to be shot out of a cannon.

All one thousand five hundred steps are torture. I try to

concentrate on one stair at a time. It is an enormous challenge. My body and mind are overloaded. Finally, I reach the seventy-fifth floor. I have done it. I finish. I have climbed to the top of the tallest building in Los Angeles.

I feel rotten. Something is wrong. I am exhausted and nauseated. My lungs feel shredded. My breath is shallow. I sit down, grab a towel and reach into my fanny pack to take out my meter, strips and lancet. I need to test my blood sugar level immediately. Two hundred seventy-four is the result. A normal person would test between 70 and 110. I drink the rest of my water and inject three units of insulin guessing at the amount I need.

I cannot celebrate. I take the elevator to the sixty-sixth floor, to the victory room, where a group is gathering while waiting for the race results. I wrap the prize, a loud large tee shirt, around my sweaty body and pace.

The reader waits as Brooke paces. Whenever she reads this piece at a public reading, every listener in the audience responds viscerally. Writing the piece, Brooke reexperienced the race. "My heart beat faster, I could feel the tension in my body, my hands began to sweat a little. I even stopped while writing to test my blood to see if the sugar levels had dropped." Her piece continues:

The results were finally in. I did the climb in twenty-three minutes, not my personal best. Not at all what I had hoped for. I got into the elevator and walked to my car in a glum mood. I drove home in silence.

My daughter called. "So Mom, how did you do?"

"Not great." I replied. "I wanted to be faster. If I did not have diabetes I would have done it so much better."

To which my wise daughter replied, "If you didn't have diabetes, you probably wouldn't climb the stairs at all."

She gathered me back together.

Intimacy

One way of achieving intimacy in memoir is to write, as Brooke did, in the present tense and to use dialogue. Most people begin memoir writing in the past tense but find that present tense creates a sense of immediacy. It was the writing of this memoir more than the running of the race that helped Brooke appreciate the enormous challenge she overcame in completing the race; it gave her a sense of pride in her stamina. And it was the conversation with her daughter that reminded her of the fact that she had accomplished a goal in spite of a disability. That short dialogue with her daughter reminds all of us of our humanity.

Another way to create intimacy in memoir is to pay very close attention to the unique vocabulary and sentence structure of your familiars. Be aware of their cadence and colloquialisms. These reveal a person's nature. Even if you can't remember dialogue of long ago word-for-word, try to get a feel for how you think the person would speak. If you start to pay close attention to those around you, chances are you will develop a good ear for remembered dialogue.

New York Times correspondent Rick Bragg captures both cadence and dialogue in writing about his northeastern Alabama family in *All Over but the Shoutin'*. When an elderly aunt died, Bragg was afraid that with the passing of each elder, the family myths and memories would be lost. So he wrote their stories and gave us their voice. He describes his father's death:

> He said he began to see a dark angel perched like a crow on the footboard of his bed, just waiting, expectant. He knew enough of the Gospel to be fearful of fallen angels, and he was afraid that it might have been dispatched from hell, special, to ferry him home. He said he threw shoes at it to get it to flutter away, but it returned, it always returned . . .
>
> He had never been inside a church in his life, back when he was young, indestructible. But as the sickness squeezed his lungs he began to hope that Jesus was more than just a fifty-cent mail-order picture enshrined in a dime-store frame on the hallway wall, the salvation was the trick card he could play right at the end and stay in the money. I know it because I asked my momma what they talked about all those times. "He talked about y'all, a little. But mostly he just wanted to talk about the Lord."

Bragg's style, his Southern rhythm and meter, as well as his daddy's physical environment with its "fifty-cent mail-order picture enshrined in a dime-store frame on the hallway wall," makes this a very intimate piece.

Tense

Most memoirs are written in first person, past tense, although some memoirists are very successful at achieving more intimacy by writing in first person, present tense. Others, like Vivian Gornick in her memoir, *Fierce Attachments,* are masters at changing tense within the same piece, even sometimes within the same paragraph.

I'm fourteen years old. It's an evening in late spring. I push open the door of Nettie's apartment. The kitchen is steeped in a kind of violet gloom, soft, full, intense. The room is empty: bathed in the lovely half-light, but empty. I stop short. The door wasn't locked, someone must be home. I walk through to the inner room. I stop on the threshold. The light is even weaker here. My eyes adjust. I see Nettie and the priest lying across the paisley-covered bed. She is naked, he is dressed. He is flat on his back. She lies half across him. His body is rigid, hers is spilling over. I can see her smiling in the half-dark.

. . . The next morning Nettie sits in a flowered house-dress at her kitchen table, mending a skirt, her face lowered, smiling to herself. She looks up at me, her green eyes falsely innocent. "Did you come in here last night?" she asks. We are all her defeated enemies this morning. Calmly I think: She hates men. . . .

When did I begin to take it in? And what did I make of it? When was the first I knew something about her in a world where men were sex, but women?—weren't we just supposed to get out of the way when we saw it coming?

In the next paragraph, Gornick describes riding her bike with her friend Marilyn three years earlier and coming across Nettie on a park bench with a man. When Marilyn informs her that Nettie is "picking up" the man, Gornick's childhood innocence is shattered. The author proceeds seamlessly from the first-person fourteen-year-old narrator speaking in present tense to the self-reflective voice of the adult written in past tense to the eleven-year-old narrator speaking in first person plural, weaving a rich tapestry of discovery.

I don't advise you to change tenses within the same piece until you have first developed skill using one tense. For most writers, it's hard to maintain cohesion in a story when verb tense is changed mid-paragraph or mid-page. Start your memoir in the past tense, and when you become more adept with verb usage, try a piece in present tense, like Gornick's: "I'm fourteen years old. It's an evening in late spring. I push open the door of Nettie's apartment."

Writing Suggestion

Now choose another episode either from your free write or another time in your life. Write a short memoir in past tense, perhaps one or two pages long. Include a description of your surroundings, who was involved, the action in the story and how you felt. Try to recall dialogue. As you write, imagine that you are having a conversation with the reader. For instance:

> It was the summer of 1970. We drove into Terre Haute, two longhairs looking for a motel room on the first night of our road trip across the country. We had left Philadelphia so that John could join a law firm in Beverly Hills. Terre Haute looked deserted; few cars were parked in front of each motel. But every innkeeper looked us up and down as we walked into the motel lobby and snarled, "No vacancy." I wondered what they were afraid of.

Now, after you have completed writing your piece, write the same event in present tense, as if it is happening right now. Notice how your writing in present tense affects your emotional response to the incident.

> It is the summer of 1970. We drive into Terre Haute looking for a motel room. It's the end of a long day of driving from Philadelphia on our way across the country. We're bushed, but we're about to embark upon a new life. John is joining a law firm in Beverly Hills. Both of us wear our hair long, but we're not hippies; we already pay taxes. The town looks empty; there are few cars parked in front of each motel, but at every front office we are told, "No vacancy." What are they afraid of?

From my two examples, you may notice that writing in past tense creates more distance from the event, whereas writing in present tense gives the event a sense of immediacy. There is more energy to the writing and it's more spontaneous, more conversational.

As you experiment with past and present tense, you'll be able to decide which is more appropriate to the telling of your particular memory. For example, Gornick describes a very intimate episode that occurs in her next-door neighbor's tiny bedroom. Her use of first person, present tense, places the reader in the scene with her, observing what she observes, feeling what she feels. She does not hesitate to reveal what she has seen. In fact, she invites the reader into her reflections: "When did I begin to take it in? And what did I make of it?" Gornick has a specific reason for revealing this incident. Her memoir is primarily about becoming a woman, and she informs the reader that she learned everything there was to learn about being a woman from two very different sources, her mother and Nettie.

When you write your memoir, pay careful attention to verb tense, relational style and intimate tone. These are effective tools to draw the reader into your memory.

Emotional Truth and the Voice of the Narrator

This is a memoir, not a history book, but in an effort to make it accurate, I've tried to check my memory against the facts. It is distressing for me to note how infrequently the facts concur with my memory of what happened. I assume, in cases like this, that the facts are wrong.

—Andy Rooney, *My War*

Emotional Truth

*A*ndy Rooney is right; memoir is not history. It's an attempt by the author to narrate her memories with the greatest emotional truth she can muster. That probably means that not every fact is completely accurate. If you're the writer, it's *your* memory of the event written from *your* perspective—not your sister's, husband's or your child's. Each of your family members may tell the story of a particular event differently because of their particular point of view, but that does not mean that your account is untrue.

As a memoirist, it is your job to relate your memory as sincerely as possible and to assure the reader that you have done a sufficient amount of reflection so that what you write is your best understanding of what originally happened. The reader cannot expect you, as writer, to remember every single detail or conversation accurately. But the reader has the right to expect that what you claim to be true will be accurate to the best of your recollection. Remember, memoir is about honesty, not about how you appear to others. If you write with emotional truth, your reader will care about you and the events in your life. Your writing will appear authentic, which is much more important than making you look good.

In an interview with William Zinsser, Toni Morrison made a great distinction between fact and truth, which I think applies here: "Fact can exist without human intelligence but truth cannot." Anyone can write facts; not everyone has the courage to write the truth, particularly about herself.

One of the steps to writing a successful memoir is to mine the emotional truth of a situation and make the reader care not only for you, as narrator, but for the people in your life as well. When you are talking about yourself, you are talking about all of us to a certain degree. As humans, we are complex creatures with many different facets to our personalities. Be careful not to describe yourself and the people in your memoir as fixed, one-dimensional characters. No reader will believe you if you present yourself *solely* as a wonderful daughter (wife, mother, sister) or son (husband, father, brother) or, on the other hand, if you present your life as one series of mishaps after another. Readers quickly lose interest in victim memoirs. Give each character their due, no matter how much you like or are repelled by them.

In *The Liars' Club,* Mary Karr describes her mother as a drunk and a bit crazy, but she also paints her with the utmost compassion and love. At age eight, Karr comes home from school one day with a perfect spelling test and runs around the house trying to find her mother to show her the paper. Instead, she finds an open letter from her grandmother's lawyer on the couch explaining the terms of her grandmother's will. Then she finds her mother outside in her painting studio, sitting in her grandmother's rocker, torching everything in sight.

> Mother's back to me in that rocker conjured that old Alfred Hitchcock movie *Psycho* she'd taken us to in 1960. In the end, the crazy killer was got up like his nutty old mother with a gray wig. He rocked in her personal chair. Mother turned around slow to face me like old Tony Perkins. Her face came into my head one sharp frame at a time. I finally saw in these instants that Mother's own face had been all scribbled up with that mud-colored lipstick. *She was trying to scrub herself out,* I thought. Sure enough, the scribbles weren't like those on an African mask or like a kid's war paint. They didn't involve the underlying face that much. They lacked form. No neat triangles or straight lines went along the planes on the face. She looked genuinely crazy sitting in her mother's rocker with the neatly ruffled blue calico cushions in front of that blazing stove with the smell of charcoal fluid and her own face all scrawled up bloody red.

Karr's memory of her mother's grief is multilayered. She doesn't ask the reader to feel sorry for her childhood self; instead she portrays actions that illustrate the very complex feelings of a woman who has just lost her mother.

Some memoirists reveal their faults to the reader as a way of exploring a deeper truth about themselves. I wrote a short memoir, "Christmas Tree Light Psychosis," about a standing joke in my family, to show the fallibility of a single parent trying to cope with her irrational need to decorate the Christmas tree perfectly. In the piece, my thirteen-year-old son volunteers to take over the task of stringing the Christmas tree lights one year, which, upon reflection, is an offer that could be seen as both foolhardy and courageous.

"Mom, I'd like to do the lights this year."

"Are you sure? You know what that means?"

"Yes, I know you want them just right and I can do them. Why don't you go upstairs and Heather and I will call you when we're done?"

So I went upstairs. And I tried to sit still. I paced from my bedroom to the bathroom and back again to the bedroom. I lay down on my bed, looked up at the ceiling and tried to breathe deeply. I considered the courage your request took. I wondered if you and Heather had planned this in private to alleviate another Christmas tree light drama or if yours had been a spontaneous gesture. I made a pact with myself that however the tree looked, it would be acceptable.

It was Heather's voice that called me downstairs. It seemed a little too soon to my mind for you to have done a careful job. But I quieted my critic and gingerly walked downstairs.

The tree was lit and it had a rakish tilt. It was clear that the lights were a-tangle. The colored lights (from the sixties) bunched up on the right side at the top of the tree and the white twinkle lights (from the seventies) drooped around the bottom. The glass balls were spaced more evenly.

"How do you like it, Mom?" said Heather. "I did the balls and Brendan did the lights."

"Yeah, I tried to give them a new look," you said. "I decided they wanted to be a bit freer this year. So I picked up the colored ones and threw them up over the top of the tree and where they landed they stayed. Looks pretty cool, doesn't it?"

I started to laugh. It did look cool. The tree looked happy—it looked like a well-licked ice cream cone that had started to melt. It was so incongruous to my obsessive light-stringing nature that it tickled me completely. I laughed so hard I started to cry. And all of a sudden, years of trying to imitate my father's tree-decorating perfectionism washed away and my psychosis was cured. At least temporarily!

I used humor in this piece to reveal my own embarrassment at being so neurotic about the perfect placement of Christmas tree lights. Remember, one of the elements of memoir is to be an authentic narrator—to be willing to expose your foibles and distortions and to laugh at yourself. The trick is to remember that you, yourself, are not that important, except in illuminating the universal traits we all share.

The Narrator's Voice

The narrator is the voice that tells the story. Most memoirs are written in first-person narration from the perspective of the personal "I." Remember, this is your life you are writing about, your ambitions, successes and, perhaps, even your failures, so begin in the first person. Write your story in such a way that the reader cares about what happens to you, the narrator. As you develop your skills as a storyteller and wordsmith, your readers will care more deeply about your memories too.

If writing in the first person is just too intimidating, try first using the third-person narrator, "she" or "he." When you become more relaxed with your own material, you may choose to change it to first-person narration.

One of my students, Anne, employed this tactic. She started a piece about her relationship with her ex-husband in one of my memoir classes and then decided to expand it to a full-length book in an ongoing memoir group. However, as she began to write about her early romance and marriage, she found that writing in the first person was too intimidating. First of all, her story involved revealing facts about herself and a man who had had some stature in their church community; additionally, she was not sure she wanted her adult daughters to know the extent of the neglect and abuse that had occurred in the marriage. She wrote the entire book in third person and used pseudonyms. It took her three years.

After Anne had completed the manuscript and digested it, she arrived at the writing group one day with the first chapter of her book completely rewritten in first-person narration, using her own name. She explained that she had needed the anonymity of third person to explore the details of her marriage, divorce and recovery. Now she was ready to claim it as *her* story.

South African novelist and critic J. M. Coetzee chose a third-person narrator in writing the second installment of his memoir

Youth. His earlier memoir, *Boyhood,* is also written in third person, present tense, and the hero is named "John," from John Michael Coetzee. While I don't know Coetzee's reason for writing in third person, his words are telling. As John turns thirteen, he becomes "surly, scowling, dark. He does not like this new ugly self, he wants to be drawn out of it, but that is something he cannot do by himself."

Writing in the third person is not an uncommon method to use at first, particularly when a memoirist is writing about a painful event that has not yet been resolved or about people who are still alive. When writing about living people, it is always important to ask, "What is my story to tell?" Each memoirist has to balance the reasons for writing a particular story or for using real names against the harm it might cause someone else.

Your options are to change the names and identifying details in your memoir, to show the person you have written about what you have written and get their approval to use it, or to refrain from making public the story until the person is dead. If a story seems too personal, it is often because it has not yet been resolved. That's why it took Anne three years of working with her material to come to terms with her memoir. If the story is not resolved, it is likely that the writer has not gained enough distance from the memory to reflect upon its meaning and is therefore asking too much of the reader. Remember, it is the job of the writer to make a memoir meaningful to the reader.

Some memoirists choose to use second-person narration. You may have noticed in my excerpt from "Christmas Tree Light Psychosis" that I directly address my young son, now a man in his thirties: "I considered the courage your request took. I wondered if you and

Heather had planned this in private to alleviate another Christmas tree light drama or if yours had been a spontaneous gesture."

This memoir was written in letter form and was inspired by a piece written by Alice Walker in *The Way Forward Is with a Broken Heart*. Walker wrote her memoir, "To My Young Husband," to the man who was the partner of her youth, from whom she had been divorced for two decades.

> You do not talk to me now, a fate I could not have imagined twenty years ago. It is true we say the usual greetings, when we have to, over the phone: How are you? Have you heard from Our child? But beyond that, really nothing. Nothing of the secrets, memories, good and bad, that we shared. Nothing of the laughter that used to creep up on us as we ate together late at night at the kitchen table—perhaps after one of your poker games—and then wash over us in a cackling wave.

Walker's use of second-person narration is both relational and intimate. When writing a strong emotional memory involving a certain person, the letter form of narration if often very effective. Because the writer is not face-to-face with the listener, the writer may be able to access a greater degree of emotional truth.

Writing Suggestion

Now that we've explored narrative style, choose an incident from your life and write it in first-person narration, using the personal

"I" (i.e., I once lived in Venice). The following example is from "Leave It to Beaver," a memoir written by my student Dorothy.

Take it from me, those who leave it to Beaver will end up with a dam and a pool of stagnating spontaneity, romance, and compassion lost. I know, because Beaver is my husband of many years. There was a time when I called that compulsive sports fan, car-nut, clothes-buff "Honey," "Dear," or just "Jack." Those endearments ended, however, when we took a ten-day riverboat trip on the beautiful Blue Danube with four additional days in Turkey. Silly me, I left it to Beaver to pack and spent thirteen days in seven countries looking for men's underwear.

Now, using the example of Alice Walker, try writing your memoir in second person as if you are writing a letter to a friend or family member. I had suggested to one of my students, Janet, that she write a memoir in letter form to her deceased husband, Richard. In "Dearest Richard," she reminisces about their romance fifty-two years ago.

Whenever the day is gray, rainy, and deeply dreamy, why do I dwell on our life so? I'm going back to your first real car, that brown and cream Chevrolet, and the time we spent in it on the weekends you drove from Michigan to Massachusetts.

You'd get there Saturday morning after driving all night through Canada to Buffalo and on to Pittsfield and South

Hadley. There were no thruways then, just highways, little towns, mountains, woods. The only room available near the college was in a boarding house on the road not far from Abbey, my dorm senior year. I never saw the inside of your room but it sounded pretty dismal.

We'd have breakfast at the College Inn and if it was rainy like today, go back to the car, drive up to the mountains and park. It always took a while before the distance between us disappeared. Maybe half the day. I couldn't feel close until I got used to the real you wearing rumpled old clothes, growing a slight beard, looking tired and anxious. It was like meeting you all over again.

Lastly, take the memoir that you have written earlier in first-person narration and try it in third person. What is your emotional reaction to the two pieces? Do you feel somewhat distanced from your own memory in third person, or is it easier to explore a particular event from some distance? Try it again in second person, as if writing a letter, and notice if the voice becomes more immediate.

Humor and Self-Reflection

Though you don't need to be a comedian and make jokes, as a memoirist you need a comic vision. Humor helps you strip away facades and expose the imperfect bare-assed truth beneath.

—Tristine Rainer, *Your Life as Story*

tressing the humorous or unexpected aspects of human nature gives memoir its vitality. The successful memoirist is not afraid to reveal her foibles and what she has learned from them. We all make mistakes we wish we could forget; some of these are hilarious. The memoirist's ability to laugh at herself helps the reader enjoy the absurd in life too.

Think about Anne Lamott discovering God in the ladies' room. She admits, "Maybe God is in the men's room too, but I have been in so few of them since I got sober." She knows how to turn a phrase to reveal her flaws in such a way that invites the reader to look at her own imperfections with amusement as well.

Memoirists often poke gentle fun at loved ones too. As I mentioned earlier, my student Dorothy wrote about the riverboat trip she and her husband took down the beautiful Blue Danube. Jack forgot to pack his underwear and Dorothy describes the trip from a shopper's point of view—looking for men's briefs in country after country throughout the Balkans.

> If one is fortunate enough to first see Budapest from the deck of a riverboat on the Danube as it glides beneath the Chain Bridge just as night falls, one is blessed with an indelible memory of incredible splendor—it's as if a necklace of lights had been strung on fairy tale castles mirrored in the oil slick flow of the Danube. I'll always remember that magic moment. My mate, on the other hand, missed it—he was sudsing his undies.

With writing, as with life, you may need distance from the event before you can find its inherent humor. Frank McCourt says that if *Angela's Ashes* had been published thirty years ago it would have been an indictment, a condemnation—humorless. But he has reached a stage in his life where he feels there's nothing for him to lose anymore, so he can laugh at himself.

In *'Tis,* he reveals his very human failures as a man and as a husband just as humorously as he points out in *Angela's Ashes* the moral complexities of being Irish and Catholic. He begins *Angela's Ashes* with: "When I look back on my childhood I wonder how I managed to survive at all. It was, of course, a miserable childhood: the happy childhood is hardly worth your while. Worse than the ordinary miserable childhood is the miserable Irish childhood, and worse yet is the miserable Irish Catholic childhood."

Such writing allows us to find perspective and playfulness in our own lives regardless of the circumstances. McCourt turned what could have been a harrowing survivor's tale filled with self-pity and retribution into a truly inspirational journey filled with spontaneity, compassion and humor.

Writing Suggestion

It doesn't matter how young or old you are when you begin to write about your life. To write with humor, make a list of all of the funny, embarrassing or unusual things that have ever happened to you. Go back to your childhood and write forward. Now choose one event and write about it from a comedic perspective. Remember to include dialogue, because it always reveals so much about the characters in your life.

Every family has at least one family member who is eccentric, odd or humorous. Write a memory about this person from your point of view, or write a story that is told at family gatherings that always gets a laugh.

Self-Reflection

The hallmark of memoir is its insight, the writer's willingness to look within and reveal her struggle to understand some aspect of her life. Life today is so fast-paced and externally focused that there is little time to reflect. Writing memoir addresses that void. As a memoirist, you are asked to disclose what you've learned along your journey.

You can either muse upon a scene, incorporating your thoughts about the event as it happens, or speculate to yourself off the page and then convey your insight. Throughout "The Table," Alyce Miller reveals her desire not only to discover the contents in the envelope taped underneath her mother's end table, but also to have her mother join her: "I imagined the two of us, conspirators, sneaking into the room where the table sat, and together peeling the envelope away and discovering the secret inside. It was something we would share, something that would bind us together." Reading this, you recognize the workings of a child's mind wanting her mother to be her best friend in larceny.

In *Paula,* Isabel Allende gazes at her terminally ill daughter and reflects upon her own life as a writer.

> When I look back, it seems to me that I was the protagonist of a melodrama; now, in contrast everything is suspended, I have nothing to tell, the present has the brutal certainty of tragedy. I close my eyes and before me rises the painful image of my daughter in her wheelchair, her eyes staring toward the sea, her gaze focused beyond the horizon where death begins.

At that moment, nothing else is important to her besides her role as mother trying desperately to keep her daughter alive.

In both of these examples, the author shares her thought processes with the reader as the story unfolds. Some authors take another approach by reflecting on what they have learned about themselves at the end of their memoir. Inga Clendinnen concludes

Tiger's Eye by reaffirming her devotion to her chosen profession, history.

> So that is what I have been doing all this time—by courtesy of a physiological malfunction, taking a journey out, beyond and around myself, and into interior territories previously closed to me. At the end of it, battered, possibly wiser, certainly wearier, and oddly, happier, I have returned to where I began: to history, with a deepened sense of what peculiar creatures we are, you and I, making our marks on paper, puzzling over the past and the present doings of our species, pursuing our peculiar passion for talking with strangers.

No matter which route you take, give the reader a glimpse into what you are discovering about yourself. Without self-reflection there is no memoir; you must examine, digest and assimilate an event to find its true meaning. Be willing to allow this process to evolve at its own pace.

Writing Suggestion

To write with reflection, ask yourself the following questions each time you finish a piece:

What do I know now that I did not know before?
How does that feel? What do I think about it?
What more do I want to find out?

Then rework the piece based on your answers. You may want to keep a separate notebook or computer file for your reflections, where you ask yourself questions, make observations and challenge yourself to go to the next level. You will find that as you become more reflective about your life, your writing will become more textured too.

Some writers finish a piece, put it away in a drawer for a week and dream on it. You may wish to do that also. Afterward, take it out, read it aloud to yourself and decide what you want to add or delete from the story.

Writing memoir will change your life; you can not remain unaffected by reliving events that happened perhaps decades ago. Memoir offers the writer catharsis, new insights and rediscovery. In *The Art of the Personal Essay,* Phillip Lopate quotes one of the first memoirists, Michel de Montaigne, who confirms this: "Painting myself for others, I have painted my inward self with colors clearer than my original ones. I have no more made my book than my book has made me." The stories we leave the next generation become the memories upon which they build their lives.

Glossary of Terms

Archetype - a preexisting pattern or imprint that forms the blueprint for the major dynamic components of the human personality

Cadence - the beat or measure of the rhythmical flow of sounds in a language

Character - the representation of a person in a work of literature

Cohesion - the quality of a story's sequence of events following smoothly and logically

Colloquial - belonging to the conversational language of everyday speech

Colloquialism - local words and expressions commonly used in particular geographical regions

Confessional Style - a story told in the manner of disclosing a shortcoming or fault of one's own

Conflict - the antagonistic state or action between incompatible ideas, interests or characters

Descriptive Language - discourse that creates a mental image for the reader

Dialogue - a conversation between two or more people in a story

Emotional Distance - the state of keeping one's feelings removed from a subject or moment

Emotional Essence - the core nature of emotions involved in a body of work

Emotional Reaction - a strong feeling and physiological response that exists in relation to a stimulus such as an event or relationship

Emotional Truth - the author's sincere feelings about an event or experience; the avoidance of distortion or misrepresentation of an event or experience

Episode - an event that is one of a series of connected stories or scenes

Figurative Language - language whose meaning is conveyed through the use of imaginative comparisons

First-Person Narration - a story told from the point of view of the author (nonfiction)

Focal Point - a central activity, attention or attraction

Humor - the ability to perceive and express the ludicrous, comical or absurdly incongruous

Imagery - the use of sensory detail to make what is being described more vivid

Incident - an action or event that occurs

Intimate Tone - language that is marked by a personal familiarity or close association

Kinesthetic Sensation - sensory experience that is stored in the body (muscles, tendons and joints) and is stimulated by emotion and physical movement

Literal Language - language that relies on the standard meanings of words

Metaphor - a comparison equating two dissimilar things based on a shared quality

Meter - the pattern of a continually repeated rhythm in verse

Mood - the writer's predominant attitude and set of emotions present in a work

Narration - the process of recounting the events in a story

Narrative - the body of literary work that is recounted

One-Dimensional Character - a flat character that has not been well developed

Person - indicates whether a person is speaking (first person), is spoken to (second person) or is spoken about (third person)

Personal "I" - the telling of a story using an intimate tone and first-person pronoun

Pivotal Event - a vitally important occurrence that has a major role, function or effect upon a story

Place - the physical environment and surroundings of an area

Point of View - the perspective from which a story is told

Relational Style - a conversational manner of expressing thought in language

Remembered Event - a recalled image or episode from the past

Resolution - the point in a literary work in which the main dramatic complication is worked out

Retrospection - the process of thinking over past events

Rhythm - the regular repetition of stressed syllables and pauses in verse

Self-Reflection - the thoughtful examination of one's actions and mindset

Sense Memories - events that are recalled through associative mechanisms such as smell, sound, taste, texture, vision and movement

Sense of Immediacy - the state or feeling relating to the here and now

Sensory Detail - description that relies on sight, sound, smell, taste and touch

Significance - the importance found in the meaning of a thing

Simile - a comparison introduced by "like" or "as," equating two dissimilar things based on a shared quality

Tension - the balance maintained between opposing elements in a body of work

Theme - a topic or idea expressed by a work of literature

Tone - the style of expression a writer uses, which reveals her attitude toward the work's subject, characters or audience

Underlying Story - the basis of a narrative that is evident upon attention to background information

Unique Vocabulary - an unusual or rare stock of words used by a language, group, individual or work in a field of knowledge

Universal Theme - a theme that is comprehensive in scope and present in all cultures

Vignette - a brief descriptive literary sketch

Voice - a distinction of verb form that indicates whether a subject acts (active) or is acted upon (passive)

Bibliography

Books

Abbott, Shirley. *The Bookmaker's Daughter: A Memory Unbound.* New York: Ticknor and Fields, 1991.

Albom, Mitch. *Tuesdays with Morrie: An Old Man, a Young Man, and Life's Greatest Lesson.* New York: Doubleday, 1997.

Alexander, Meena. *Fault Lines: A Memoir.* New York: Feminist Press, 1993.

Allende, Isabel. *Paula.* New York: HarperCollins, 1996.

Atwood, Margaret. *The Blind Assassin.* New York: Doubleday, 2000.

Barrington, Judith. *Writing the Memoir: From Truth to Art.* Portland, Ore.: Eighth Mountain Press, 1997.

Bauby, Jean-Dominique. *The Diving Bell and the Butterfly.* New York: Vintage International, 1998.

Bayley, John. *Elegy for Iris.* New York: St. Martin's Press, 1999.

Bragg, Rick. *All Over but the Shoutin'.* New York: Pantheon Books, 1997.

Cheever, Susan. *Note Found in a Bottle: My Life as a Drinker.* New York: Simon & Schuster, 1999.

Chernin, Kim. *In My Mother's House.* New York: Harper & Row, 1983.

Clendinnen, Inga. *Tiger's Eye: A Memoir.* New York: Scribner, 2001.

Coetzee, J. M. *Boyhood: Scenes from Provincial Life*. New York: Viking, 1997.

———. *Youth: Scenes from Provincial Life II*. New York: Viking, 2002.

Conway, Jill Ker. *The Road from Coorain*. New York: Vintage, 1990.

———. *True North: A Memoir*. New York: Vintage, 1994.

———. *When Memory Speaks: Reflections on Autobiography*. New York: Alfred A. Knopf, 1998.

———. *A Woman's Education*. New York: Alfred A. Knopf, 2001.

———, ed. *Written by Herself: Women's Memoirs from Britain, Africa, Asia and the United States*. New York: Vintage, 1996.

Delattre, Pierre. *Episodes*. St. Paul, Minn.: Graywolf Press, 1993.

DeSalvo, Louise. *Writing as a Way of Healing: How Telling Our Stories Transforms Our Lives*. Boston: Beacon Press, 2000.

Diski, Jenny. *Skating to Antarctica*. Hopewell, N. J.: Ecco Press, 1998.

Eggers, Dave. *A Heartbreaking Work of Staggering Genius*. New York: Vintage, 2001.

Fernandez Barrios, Flor. *Blessed by Thunder: Memoir of a Cuban Girlhood*. Seattle: Seal Press, 1999.

Frazer, Sir James George. *The Golden Bough*. London: Macmillan and Co., 1950.

Frazier, Ian. *Family*. New York: HarperPerennial, 1995.

Gates, Henry Louis, Jr. *Colored People: A Memoir*. New York: Vintage, 1995.

Gordon, Emily Fox. *Mockingbird Years: A Life In and Out of Therapy*. New York: Basic Books, 2000.

Gordon, Mary. *The Shadow Man: A Daughter's Search for Her Father*. New York: Vintage, 1997.

Gornick, Vivian. *Fierce Attachments: A Memoir*. New York: Simon & Schuster, 1988.

———. *The Situation and the Story*. New York: Farrar, Straus & Giroux, 2001.

Greer, Germaine. *Daddy, We Hardly Knew You*. New York: Alfred A. Knopf, 1990.

Griffin, Susan. *A Chorus of Stones*. New York: Anchor Books, 1993.

Hahn, Hannelore. *On the Way to Feed the Swans: A Memoir*. New York: Tenth House, 1982.

Hampl, Patricia. *I Could Tell You Stories: Sojourns in the Land of Memory*. New York: W. W. Norton & Co., 1999.

Harrison, Kathryn. *The Kiss: A Memoir*. New York: Random House, 1997.

Heilbrun, Carolyn G. *Writing a Woman's Life*. New York: Ballantine Books, 1989.

———. *Hamlet's Mother and Other Women*. New York: Ballantine Books, 1991.

Hollis, James. *The Archetypal Imagination*. College Station: Texas A&M University Press, 2000.

hooks, bell. *Remembered Rapture: The Writer at Work*. New York: Henry Holt & Co., 1999.

Hornbacher, Marya. *Wasted: A Memoir of Anorexia and Bulimia*. New York: HarperCollins, 1998.

Jacobs, Harriet A. *Incidents in the Life of a Slave Girl: Written by Herself*. Cambridge, Mass.: Harvard University Press, 2000.

Jamison, Kay Redfield. *An Unquiet Mind*. New York: Alfred A. Knopf, 1995.

Kamenetz, Rodger. *Terra Infirma: A Memoir of My Mother's Life in Mine*. New York: Schocken Books, 1998.

Kaplan, Alice. *French Lessons: A Memoir*. Chicago: University of Chicago Press, 1993.

Karr, Mary. *The Liars' Club: A Memoir*. New York: Penguin Books, 1995.

————. *Cherry: A Memoir*. New York: Viking Penguin, 2000.

King, Stephen. *On Writing: A Memoir of the Craft*. New York: Scribner, 2000.

Kingston, Maxine Hong. *The Woman Warrior: Memoirs of a Girlhood Among Ghosts*. New York: Vintage, 1989.

Knapp, Caroline. *Drinking: A Love Story*. New York: Delta, 1997.

Lamott, Anne. *Bird by Bird: Some Instructions on Writing and Life*. New York: Pantheon Books, 1994.

————. *Traveling Mercies: Some Thoughts on Faith*. New York: Random House, 1999.

Lopate, Phillip. *The Art of the Personal Essay*. New York: Anchor Books, 1995.

Lyden, Jacki. *Daughter of the Queen of Sheba*. New York: Penguin Books, 1998.

MacDonald, Michael Patrick. *All Souls: A Family Story from Southie*. Boston: Beacon Press, 1999.

Mayer, Musa. *Night Studio: A Memoir of Philip Guston*. New York: Alfred A. Knopf, 1988.

————. *Examining Myself: One Woman's Story of Breast Cancer Treatment and Recovery*. New York: Faber & Faber, 1994.

McBride, James. *The Color of Water: A Black Man's Tribute to His White Mother*. New York: Riverhead Books, 1996.

McCarthy, Mary. *Memories of a Catholic Girlhood*. New York: Harcourt Brace Jovanovich, 1957.

McConkey, James, ed. *The Anatomy of Memory*. New York: Oxford University Press, 1996.

McCourt, Frank. *Angela's Ashes: A Memoir*. New York: Scribner, 1996.

———. *'Tis: A Memoir*. New York: Touchstone, 2000.

Menchú, Ribogerta. *I, Rigoberta Menchú: An Indian Woman in Guatemala*. London: Verso, 1984.

Merriman, Andy. *A Minor Adjustment: The Story of Sarah, a Remarkable Child*. London: Pan Books, 1999.

Murdock, Maureen. *The Heroine's Journey: Woman's Quest for Wholeness*. Boston: Shambhala, 1990.

———. *Fathers' Daughters: Transforming the Father-Daughter Relationship*. New York: Fawcett, 1996.

———, ed. *Monday Morning Memoirs: Women in the Second Half of Life*. Philadelphia: Xlibris, 2002.

Norris, Kathleen. *Dakota: A Spiritual Geography*. Boston: Houghton Mifflin, 2001.

O'Faolain, Nuala. *Are You Somebody?: The Accidental Memoir of a Dublin Woman*. New York: Henry Holt, 1998.

O'Reilley, Mary Rose. *The Barn at the End of the World: The Apprenticeship of a Quaker, Buddhist Shepherd*. Minneapolis: Milkweed, 2000.

Peterson, Brenda. *Sister Stories: Taking the Journey Together*. New York: Viking, 1996.

Rainer, Tristine. *Your Life as Story: Discovering the "New Autobiography" and Writing Memoir as Literature*. New York: Tarcher/Putnam, 1998.

Reichl, Ruth. *Tender at the Bone: Growing Up at the Table*. New York: Random House, 1998.

———. *Comfort Me with Apples: More Adventures at the Table*. New York: Random House, 2001.

Roberts, Cokie. *We Are Our Mothers' Daughters*. New York: William Morrow, 1998.

Rooney, Andy. *My War*. New York: Public Affairs, 2000.

Sarton, May. *Journal of a Solitude*. New York: W. W. Norton & Co., 1973.

See, Carolyn. *Dreaming: Hard Luck and Good Times in America*. New York: Random House, 1995.

Simpson, Eileen. *Poets in Their Youth: A Memoir*. New York: Random House, 1982.

Slater, Lauren. *Welcome to My Country*. New York: Anchor Books, 1997.

———. *Lying: A Metaphorical Memoir*. New York: Random House, 2000.

Tiberghien, Susan M. *Looking for Gold: A Year in Jungian Analysis*. Einsiedeln, Switzerland: Daimon Verlag, 1995.

———. *Circling to the Center: One Woman's Encounter with Silent Prayer*. New York: Paulist Press, 2000.

Walker, Alice. *The Way Forward Is with a Broken Heart*. New York: Random House, 2000.

Walker, Rebecca. *Black, White and Jewish: Autobiography of a Shifting Self*. New York: Riverhead Books, 2001.

Welch, John. *Spiritual Pilgrims: Carl Jung and Teresa of Avila*. New York: Paulist Press, 1982.

Wilde-Menozzi, Wallis. *Mother Tongue: An American Life in Italy*. New York: North Point Press, 1997.

Williams, Terry Tempest. *Refuge: An Unnatural History of Family and Place*. New York: Vintage Books, 1992.

————. *Leap*. New York: Pantheon, 2000.

Wolff, Geoffrey. *The Duke of Deception: Memories of My Father*. New York: Vintage Books, 1990.

Young-Bruehl, Elisabeth. *Subject to Biography: Psychoanalysis, Feminism, and Writing Women's Lives*. Cambridge, Mass.: Harvard University Press, 1998.

Zinsser, William, ed. *Inventing the Truth: The Art and Craft of Memoir*. Boston: Houghton Mifflin, 1998.

Articles

Miller, Alyce. "The Table." *Fourth Genre,* Vol. 2, No. 2, 2000.

Murdock, Maureen. "Telling Our Stories: Making Meaning from Myth and Memoir." Dennis Slattery and Lionel Corbett, eds. *Depth Psychology: Meditations in the Field*. Einsiedeln: Daimon Verlag and Pacifica Graduate Institute, 2000.

Ventura, Michael. "The Mission of Memory." *The Family Networker* 20(6), 1996.

Acknowledgments

Like all writers who attempt to explore the truth of their memories, I draw on the courage and skill of memoirists from all times, particularly the women and men who have written their lives in the last century. As a teacher, I would not be in the fortunate position of reading memoirs and teaching creative nonfiction without the support of the UCLA Extension Writers' Program and the many students I have had the privilege to work with over the last thirteen years, particularly the stalwarts in the Monday morning group, Brooke Anderson, Ruth Bracken, Ruth Bochner, Jackie Connolly, Bairbre Dowling, Hillary Horan, Dorothy Huebel, Marilyn Kierscey and Janet Smith. My thanks to the writers in the International Womens' Writing Guild; my Wednesday morning group, Genevieve Neuman, Alice Gillaroo, Deb Clayton, Rachel Altman, Monique Fay, Michele Gardner-Smith, Dorothy Boswell, Nancy Kawalek, Sue Colin and Mary DiMeglio; and my students at Pacifica Graduate Institute, all who have dared to write their lives.

As a writer, I have been blessed with two women who nurtured this project from the start, Leslie Miller at Seal Press, who has been a delightful and insightful editor, and my agent, Felicia Eth. The Ledig-Rowohlt Foundation in Switzerland awarded me a writing residency at the Chateau de Lavigny International Writer's Colony in 1999, where I began this book in the "Nabokov" room and Pacifica

Graduate Institute gave me a three-month sabbatical to clear my head. My writing buddy, Susan King, drove up to Santa Barbara every other month from Los Angeles to encourage me to dig deeper—without her vigilance, I would have been a more slippery narrator. Thanks also to my friend Dennis Slattery, who read early chapters; my daughter, Heather Murdock, who read later ones; Susan Tiberghien, Flor Fernandez Barrios, Lonny Shavelson and Chris Downing for good conversations about the art of memoir writing; Dianne Skafte, Edie Barrett and Ginette Paris for their vision and faith; and Bill Dial for his love and support. Finally, thanks to my mother, father and sister for their patience with my view of our lives.

Credits

Grateful acknowledgment is made to the following publishers for the right to excerpt material:

Excerpts from *Paula* by Isabel Allende. Copyright © 1994 by Isabel Allende. Used by permission of HarperCollins Publishers.

Excerpts from *Blessed by Thunder* by Flor Fernandez Barrios. Copyright © 1998 by Flor Fernandez Barrios. Used with permission of Seal Press.

Excerpts from *Elegy for Iris* by John Bayley. Copyright © 1999 by John Bayley. Reprinted by permission of St. Martin's Press, LLC.

Excerpt from *All Over but the Shoutin'* by Rick Bragg. Copyright © 1997 by Rick Bragg. Used by permission of Pantheon Books, a division of Random House, Inc.

Excerpt from *In My Mother's House* by Kim Chernin. Copyright © 1983 by Kim Chernin. Reprinted by permission of Houghton Mifflin Company. All rights reserved.

Excerpt from *Tiger's Eye* by Inga Clendinnen. Copyright © 2000 by Inga Clendinnon. Reprinted with permission of Scribner, a Division of Simon & Schuster.

Excerpt from *Episodes*. Copyright © 1993 by Pierre Delattre reprinted with permission of Graywolf Press.

Excerpts from *Skating to Antarctica* by Jenny Diski. Copyright

© 1997 by Jenny Diski. Used by permission of HarperCollins Publishers.

Excerpt from *A Chorus of Stones* by Susan Griffin. Copyright © 1992 by Susan Griffin. Used with permission of Doubleday, a division of Random House, Inc.

Excerpts from *Fierce Attachments* by Vivian Gornick. Copyright © 1987 by Vivian Gornick. Reprinted by permission of Farrar, Straus and Giroux, LLC.

Excerpt from "Chapter 7" from *The Liars' Club* by Mary Karr. Copyright © 1995 by Mary Karr. Used by permission of Viking Penguin, a division of Penguin Putnam Inc.

Excerpt from *Traveling Mercies* by Anne Lamott. Copyright © 1999 by Anne Lamott. Used by permission of Pantheon Books, a division of Random House, Inc.

Excerpts from *Daughter of the Queen of Sheba: A Memoir* by Jacki Lyden. Copyright © 1997 by Jacki Lyden. Reprinted by permission of Houghton Mifflin Company. All rights reserved.

Excerpts from *The Color of Water* by James McBride. Copyright © 1996 by James McBride. Published by Riverhead Books. Used with permission of Penguin Putnam, Inc.

Excerpts from *Dakota* by Kathleen Norris. Copyright © 1993 by Kathleen Norris. Reprinted by permission of Houghton Mifflin Company. All rights reserved.

Excerpt from *Are You Somebody?: The Accidental Memoir of a Dublin Woman* by Nuala O'Faolain. Copyright © 1998 by Nuala O'Faolain. Reprinted by permission of Henry Holt & Co., LLC.

Excerpt from *The Barn at the End of the World: The Apprenticeship of a Quaker, Buddhist Shepherd* by Mary Rose O'Reilley.

Copyright © 2000 by Mary Rose O'Reilley. Reprinted with permission from Milkweed Editions.

Excerpt from *Tender at the Bone* by Ruth Reichl. Copyright © 1998. Used with permission of Random House, Inc.

Excerpt from *Journal of a Solitude* by May Sarton. Copyright © 1973 by May Sarton. Used by permission of W.W. Norton & Company, Inc.

Excerpt from *Lying* by Lauren Slater. Copyright © 2000 by Lauren Slater. Used with permission of Random House, Inc.

Excerpts from *Circling to the Center* by Susan Tiberghien. Copyright © 2000 by Susan Tiberghien. Used with permission of Paulist Press.

Excerpt from *The Way Forward is with a Broken Heart* by Alice Walker. Copyright © 2000 by Alice Walker. Used with permission of Random House, Inc.

Excerpt from *Leap* by Terry Tempest Williams. Copyright © 2000 by Terry Tempest Williams. Used with permission of Random House, Inc.

Excerpt from *The Duke of Deception* by Geoffrey Wolff, copyright © 1990 by Geoffrey Wolff, is used with permission of Random House, Inc.

Excerpt from "The Table" by Alyce Miller originally appeared in *Fourth Genre* Vol. 2, No. 2, 2000, published by Michigan State University Press. Used with permission of Michigan State University Press.

Excerpt from "The Stairclimb" by Brooke Anderson, copyright © 2002 by Brooke Anderson, in *Monday Morning Memoirs,* reprinted with permission of the author. Excerpt from "Leave It to Beaver" by

Dorothy Huebel, copyright © 2002, in *Monday Morning Memoirs,* used with permission of the author. Excerpt from "Imprints" by Jackie Connolly, copyright © 2002, in *Monday Morning Memoirs* used with permission of the author. Excerpt from "Dear Richard" by Janet Smith, copyright © 2002, published in *Monday Morning Memoirs* used with permission of the author.

Excerpt from unpublished memoir by Rachel Altman, copyright © 2002, reprinted with permission of the author.

Excerpt from unpublished memoir by Alice Gillaroo, copyright © 2002, reprinted with permission of the author.

About the Author

Maureen Murdock was born in New York and grew up in advertising. She is a psychotherapist, writing teacher and author of the best-selling book *The Heroine's Journey: Woman's Quest for Wholeness,* as well as *Fathers' Daughters; Spinning Inward: Using Guided Imagery with Children* and *The Heroine's Journey Workbook.* Her books have been translated into a dozen languages, and she is the editor of *Monday Morning Memoirs: Women in the Second Half of Life.* A faculty member at Pacifica Graduate Institute, Murdock lives in Oakland and has two adult children.

Selected Titles from Seal Press

East T ... Watkins.
$14.95 ... iage, the
author

No Hu ... nconven-
tional ... 5-045-X.
The in ... her time,
who w

The B ... $15.95,
1-5800 ... eing the
unpaid ... e of one
Ameri

The C ... r's vivid
accoun

The Bo ...)77-8. A
brillian ... oxing.

Deser ... Binney.
$14.9 ... ets off
into t ... irnals.

The C ... *plored*
the C ... inchet,
forew ... a pio-
neerii ... wenty-
five fe ... imers.

Seal F ... s.

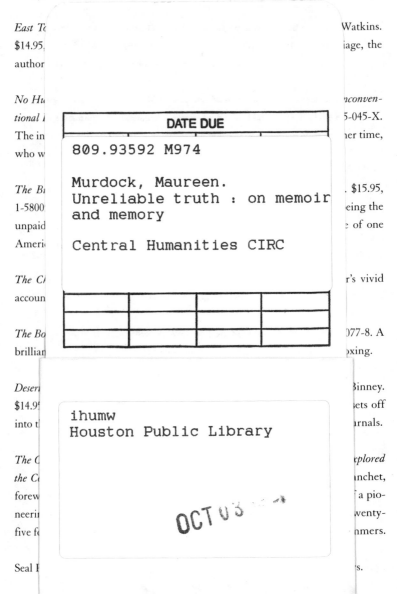

DATE DUE

809.93592 M974

Murdock, Maureen.
Unreliable truth : on memoir
and memory

Central Humanities CIRC

ihumw
Houston Public Library

OCT 03